NEW TESTAMENT STUDIES

A HEART OPENED WIDE

STUDIES IN II CORINTHIANS

HOMER A. KENT, JR.

BAKER BOOK HOUSE
Grand Rapids, Michigan 49506

Copyright 1982 by
Baker Book House Company

ISBN: 0-8010-5438-9

Printed in the United States of America

To Carrie
with a grandfather's love,
and much prayer
that you will grow to love the Savior
II Corinthians 8:9

Contents

Greeting and Thanksgiving (1:1-11)

Paul's Relations with the Corinthians (1:12—7:16)

The Collection for the
Poor Christians in Jerusalem (8–9)

Paul's Apostolic Authority (10–13)

Illustrations

The time chart is adapted from James L. Boyer's "New Testament Chronological Chart" (Winona Lake, IN: revised, 1962).

All photographs are by the author.

Abbreviations

Arndt	*A Greek-English Lexicon of the New Testament,* by William F. Arndt and F. Wilbur Gingrich
ASV	American Standard Version, 1901
EGT	*The Expositor's Greek Testament*
KJV	King James Version, 1611
LXX	Septuagint (Greek translation of the Old Testament)
NASB	New American Standard Bible, 1971
Nestle	Novum Testamentum Graece
NIV	New International Version, 1973
TDNT	*Theological Dictionary of the New Testament*

Foreword

Theological debate, the subtle influence of false teachers, unjustified gossip, and questions about apostolic authority all constitute the essense of the Second Epistle to the Corinthians.

Nowhere are the agonizing burdens of the apostle Paul more apparent than in this epistle written to a church that seemed to be in a continuous state of strife and division.

While I Corinthians has received attention by expositors, the second epistle of Paul has not been so treated, and this is unfortunate indeed. The present volume, therefore, meets an important need in New Testament studies.

This carefully written exposition of II Corinthians by my colleague, Dr. Homer A. Kent, Jr., represents a scholarly, well-balanced commentary, which is enriched by his broad knowledge of the ancient Near East, including its geography, literature, and archaeology.

Students will appreciate the informal yet accurate writing style which reflects Dr. Kent's rapport with students during many years of successful teaching in the department of New Testament and Greek at Grace Theological Seminary. Readers will also benefit from the well-balanced presentation of divergent views on various critical problems. The Greek text is handled with superb clarity and will prove useful to those who do not read

Greek, as well as to the student of Greek. The inclusion of charts, maps, and photographs also enhances the value of this book.

A careful reading of *A Heart Opened Wide* will produce a deep understanding of the apostle Paul as a man, as well as an evangelist and theologian. Dr. Kent's emphasis on matters of practical Christian living and holiness makes this commentary a valuable tool for pastor and layman alike. Serious study of this exposition, along with the text of II Corinthians, is sure to produce a new and fresh understanding of the apostle Paul, and more importantly, of the Lord Jesus Christ whom he served.

John J. Davis

Preface

Paul's Second Epistle to the Corinthians has not always fared well in translation. Some of the older English versions, in their attempt to achieve accuracy, have rendered Paul's emotional passages with such wooden literalness that the meaning is obscured if not lost altogether for modern readers. Partly for this reason, II Corinthians is not as familiar to most Christians as I Corinthians. Furthermore, the systematic discussion of problems which characterized I Corinthians has captured the attention of most students, and has tended to overshadow its companion letter.

Yet II Corinthians is worthy of serious study. Of all Paul's letters, this one is the most revealing about the author himself. His ties to his readers were strong. A number of prior contacts between him and the Corinthians had occurred, not all of which are known to us. We must read between the lines, reconstruct the setting with due caution, and then be sensitive to the nuances which are there for the discerning reader. Through the remarkable glimpse of Paul which this epistle conveys, the reader can see what it really means to minister to others. The letter is the result of a "heart opened wide" (II Cor. 6:11).

The writer of this study was assisted in his efforts by two faculty colleagues—John J. Davis and James L. Boyer—who read the manuscript and made helpful suggestions. Special thanks go also to John Davis for writing the foreword.

Homer A. Kent, Jr.
Winona Lake, Indiana

13

Introduction

Some letters are born out of careful reflection and precise planning; others spring from deep emotion. The apostle Paul wrote both kinds. His epistle to the Romans is an example of the former; II Corinthians is a product of the latter. When the apostle penned his second canonical epistle to the Corinthians, he was writing with a mixture of elation and deep concern, of personal defense coupled with generous understanding and praise. This beautiful letter is the most personal and revealing document we have from Paul's pen, for it uncovers the affectionate warmth of the man while at the same time showing the anguish of heart which he often suffered.

Nevertheless, II Corinthians has not received as much attention as its companion, I Corinthians. The variety of problems discussed in the first epistle usually captures the student's interest, and little time is left for examining its sequel. Yet the church would be the loser if it did not possess II Corinthians. Its contents are worthy of careful study.

The Church at Corinth

The nucleus of the church at Corinth was a group of Jews from the synagogue whom Paul had won to the Christian faith on his second missionary journey (Acts 18:4-8). It was soon necessary, however, for the group to leave the synagogue, and these Christians continued their

15

meetings in the home of a Gentile God-fearer named Titius Justus (Acts 18:7). It was not long before the church became predominantly Gentile (I Cor. 12:2), mostly from the lower class (I Cor. 1:26). Many members had backgrounds of gross immorality (I Cor. 6:9-11).

A variety of problems characterized this congregation, and those problems were discussed in some detail in I Corinthians. Such matters as factionalism, immorality (specifically, the behavior of church members), lawsuits against fellow Christians, marriage problems, liberty and license, church order, and spiritual gifts were given much-needed explanation. Furthermore, certain Jewish teachers (II Cor. 11:22), called by Paul "false apostles" (11:13), had infiltrated the church and sought to discredit Paul and to impose Jewish practices on the believers.

In spite of its disturbances the church at Corinth was an exciting congregation, rich in potential and thrilling in its concentration of transformed lives that reflected the power of God (I Cor. 6:11). Small wonder that Paul felt so deeply about the Corinthians and unburdened his heart in this beautiful epistle.

The Background of II Corinthians

The two canonical epistles to the Corinthians, coupled with the narrative in Acts, contain information suggesting that Paul's contacts with the church at Corinth may have been more numerous than is commonly supposed. Many interpreters[1] agree that seven contacts are properly deduced from the biblical data at hand. (1) The founding visit, at which Paul established the church at Corinth, took place during his second missionary journey (Acts 18:1-18). (2) A "lost letter" was written by Paul, dealing with the church's responsibility toward its sinning brethren (I Cor. 5:9). This letter is no longer extant, but its contents were summarized and clarified in I Corinthians 5:9-13. Word then came to Paul from the household of Chloe (I Cor. 1:11) and from Apollos (I Cor. 16:12) regarding the Corinthians. He also received a letter from the church (I Cor. 7:1), perhaps

1. See Donald Guthrie, *New Testament Introduction, The Pauline Epistles*, pp. 47-61; Murray J. Harris, "2 Corinthians," *The Expositor's Bible Commentary*, X, 307-311.

delivered by Stephanas, Fortunatus, and Achaicus (I Cor. 16:17). Paul sent Timothy to Macedonia and then on to Corinth (Acts 19:22; I Cor. 4:17) to assist in their problems, but was not sure whether Timothy would arrive before or after the church would receive I Corinthians.

(3) I Corinthians was written from Ephesus (I Cor. 16:8) on Paul's third missionary journey (I Cor. 16:8). Some of the problems must have continued, however, requiring further action. (4) A "painful visit" was undertaken by Paul from Ephesus to Corinth (II Cor. 2:1). This visit is not mentioned in Acts, but seems to be required by the data in II Corinthians. Paul refers to his next "coming" as his third one (II Cor. 12:14, 21; 13:1-2). "Comings" refer to actual visits whenever Paul mentions them, and are clearly distinguished from "coming" by letter only. This visit seems to have been unsuccessful.

(5) Returning to Ephesus, Paul wrote a "severe letter" (II Cor. 2:4, 9; 7:8-12), which Titus carried (II Cor. 12:18). It is difficult to identify this letter as I Corinthians because that epistle does not bear the marks of one composed "with many tears" (II Cor. 2:4). Nor does it seem likely that the apostle would have regretted sending a letter which was divinely inspired (II Cor. 7:8). Being impatient for Titus' return, Paul left Ephesus for Troas and then went to Macedonia where he finally met Titus and received good news (II Cor. 2:12-13; 7:5-16). (6) It was then that Paul wrote II Corinthians from Macedonia (II Cor. 8:1; 9:2-4). (7) Another visit to Corinth was undertaken, where Paul spent the three winter months (Acts 20:1-4; II Cor. 12:14; 13:1).

From the epistle itself one concludes that the place of writing was probably Macedonia, following Paul's meeting with Titus (2:13; 7:5-6). Obviously it was not written earlier than this. Announcement that Paul's visit to Corinth was shortly to occur places the writing before that event (12:14; 13:1). Inasmuch as Macedonia was adjacent to Achaia, of which Corinth was the capital, and there are several references in the letter to recent happenings in Macedonia, such a location seems almost certain (8:1; 9:2-4). The exact site is not known, although a concluding note in certain early manuscripts identifying the place of origination as

Philippi is certainly plausible.[2] Titus probably delivered the epistle (8:16-17).

A date some months after the writing of I Corinthians is likely. Inasmuch as the winter months prior to the spring feast of unleavened bread were spent at Corinth (Acts 20:1-6)—a circumstance still in the future at the time of writing—it is reasonable to place the time of writing in the fall, probably A.D. 55 (see time chart, Fig. 1).

The reasons for writing this epistle can be gleaned from its contents. Four matters appear to have provided the occasion for writing at this particular time: Titus' encouraging report, prompting Paul to a special effort to reestablish warm personal relations with the church at Corinth; a need to defend his apostleship against false teachers who had infiltrated the church; necessity for further instruction regarding the collection; and Paul's impending visit to Corinth.

The Unity of II Corinthians

The Pauline authorship of II Corinthians is not seriously disputed in scholarly circles today. No objective or documentary evidence has come forth to give any substantial reasons for doubting that this epistle came from the pen and heart of Paul. Its canonical status has unquestioned support from the earliest times.[3]

Whether the present format of the epistle represents the original structure, however, has been disputed. Did II Corinthians originally appear as we know it, or is its present form an editor's joining of several letters? Some scholars have questioned various passages,[4] but most of the attention has focused on II Corinthians 10-13. The abrupt change in tone from elation and warm expressions of love to a sustained denunciation with its uncertainty as to whether the problems at Corinth were over is the chief factor

2. Found in B^c K L P 642, and several ancient versions. Bruce M. Metzger, *A Textual Commentary on the Greek New Testament*, p. 588.

3. II Corinthians was included in Marcion's canon of around A.D. 140, and in the Muratorian canon of A.D. 170.

4. A concise resumé is given by Harris, "2 Corinthians," pp. 303-306.

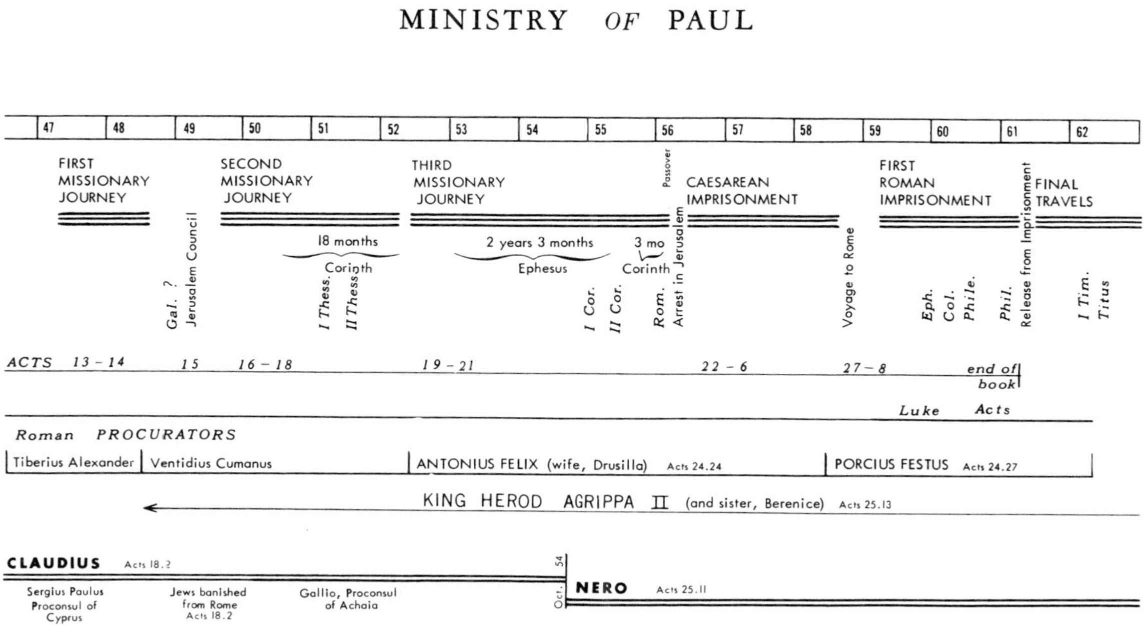

MINISTRY *OF* PAUL

47	48	49	50	51	52	53	54	55	56	57	58	59	60	61	62

FIRST MISSIONARY JOURNEY

SECOND MISSIONARY JOURNEY

THIRD MISSIONARY JOURNEY

Passover

CAESAREAN IMPRISONMENT

FIRST ROMAN IMPRISONMENT

Release from Imprisonment

FINAL TRAVELS

Gal. ?
Jerualem Council

18 months
Corinth
I Thess.
II Thess.

2 years 3 months
Ephesus

3 mo
Corinth
I Cor.
II Cor.
Rom.
Arrest in Jerusalem

Voyage to Rome

Eph.
Col.
Phile.
Phil.

I Tim.
Titus

ACTS   13 – 14   15   16 – 18   19 – 21   22 – 6   27 – 8   end of book

Luke   Acts

Roman PROCURATORS

Tiberius Alexander	Ventidius Cumanus	ANTONIUS FELIX (wife, Drusilla) Acts 24.24	PORCIUS FESTUS Acts 24.27

KING HEROD AGRIPPA II (and sister, Berenice)   Acts 25.13

CLAUDIUS   Acts 18.2

Oct. 54

NERO   Acts 25.11

Sergius Paulus Proconsul of Cyprus	Jews banished from Rome Acts 18.2	Gallio, Proconsul of Achaia

Fig. 1   Time Chart.

seized on by those who question the unity of the epistle. If chapters 1-13 are a unity, why would Paul convey the impression in 1-9 that the problem was solved, and then in 10-13 imply that it was still very much present? Many scholars argue that 1-9 are the beginning of one letter, and 10-13 are the ending of another, perhaps of the "severe letter" of 2:4.

Good reasons exist, however, for accepting the integrity of II Corinthians as it stands, and evangelical scholars have overwhelmingly done so. Among these reasons the following are convincing to this writer. First, manuscript history supports the unity of II Corinthians. No evidence has been discovered to support the notion that the present epistle ever existed as separate documents. There seems to have been no doubt regarding its unity until modern times. Second, a structural unity connects the entire letter. The author explains how he had gone from Ephesus to Macedonia, en route to a third visit to Corinth. Although he was pleased with the more wholesome attitudes at Corinth, he still recognized the presence in the church of innuendoes against him (1:17; 4:2), and these were discussed at greater length in the concluding chapters. The letter was designed to clear away problems (as much as possible) so that nothing would mar his forthcoming visit. Third, none of the partition theories are convincing. Identifying chapters 10-13 as the "severe letter" encounters the objection that those chapters are not tearful as the "severe letter" was (2:4). Paul himself seems to have been alerting his readers to the change in tone in chapters 10-13 by his opening words at 10:1. One may well understand that chapters 1-9 have laid the foundation for 10-13. Once it was clear that Paul's words were not the product of personal animosity toward the Corinthians, they would be more likely to heed his warnings against the continued presence of false teachers among them.

Outline of II Corinthians

   I. Greeting and Thanksgiving (1:1-11)
      A. The Author (1:1a)
         1. His Position
         2. His Associate

GREETING AND THANKSGIVING

(II Corinthians 1:1–11)

1

Suffering—
from God's Perspective

II Corinthians 1:1–11

How does one begin a letter when relations between the parties have been strained? What does one say when mistreatment has occurred, and previous overtures at reconciliation have been brushed aside? This was Paul's situation as he undertook the writing of II Corinthians. He could not turn his back on the Corinthians, for his love for them was deep, his investment in their spiritual lives was great, and the issues involved had far-reaching implications for them and their church. The opening remarks in this crucial letter would set the tone which could mean success or failure as to the Corinthians' response.

When Paul wrote II Corinthians, he had some reason for optimism. He had just encountered Titus, who had brought him good news from Corinth. This breakthrough in the unhappy tension between the Corinthian church and Paul put the anguish he had suffered in an entirely new light. He now recognized that God had used this suffering as an opportunity to minister His gracious comfort, and to enable him to be a better comforter of others in trouble. With this wholesome frame of mind, Paul wrote the beautiful letter that we call II Corinthians.

I. Greeting and Thanksgiving (1:1–11)

A. *The Author (1:1a)*

1. His position

VERSE 1. Paul followed the usual pattern of early letters as he first named himself, then the addressees, and afterward gave a word of greeting. Paul identified himself to his readers by the designation "apostle of Christ Jesus" and amplified it further with the words "by the will of God." This is very similar to the wording in I Corinthians, and is exactly the same as his introductions in Ephesians, Colossians, and II Timothy. It was appropriate for Paul to use this title, not only because it accurately designated him as one commissioned by Christ with an authority which only our Lord could bestow, but also because his apostolic authority had been questioned in Corinth, and would be defended later in the epistle.

Paul's position as an apostle of Christ Jesus was not self-chosen but was bestowed "by the will of God." His Corinthian readers would have been well aware of the circumstances of his conversion and call to apostleship, for he had spent a year and a half with them on his first visit (Acts 18:11), allowing abundant opportunity for his testimony to be heard and his spiritual credentials examined. It was by divine intervention that he had been transformed from the archpersecutor of the church into its greatest apologist and missionary; only the will of God was a sufficient motivator to explain Paul's willingness to undergo the sufferings he experienced and to sustain him through his trials.

2. His associate

Timothy is joined with Paul in the introduction under the simple designation "our brother." The fact that Paul was careful not to grant apostleship to Timothy, even though there was no ready alternative title except for the rather general "brother," argues for an extremely restricted view of the title "apostle of Christ Jesus" in Paul's understanding. Apparently he understood that title to designate only those who had been directly chosen by Christ Himself (see Paul's description of his authority in

Gal. 1:1, 11-24). It is a matter of record that the New Testament refers to no one other than the Twelve and Paul as an "apostle of Christ Jesus."

To call Timothy "our brother," however, was to use a term that was rich in its implications. Although Timothy's mother was Jewish and his father was Greek (Acts 16:1), he had been born again with God as his spiritual Father, and hence was a brother in the highest sense to Paul and every other believer.

It was often Paul's custom to include various associates in the opening lines of his letters, not because they were coauthors (for they were not, as the frequent use of "I" in this letter makes clear), but as a courtesy to these helpful workers. As for Timothy, he was well known to the Corinthians, having been there, along with Silas, during Paul's founding visit (Acts 18:5; II Cor. 1:19), and probably on at least one subsequent occasion (I Cor. 4:17; 16:10). He had not been mentioned in the salutation of I Corinthians because he was already on his way to Corinth. Whether that visit had been a pleasant one for Timothy can only be conjectured. It does seem probable that his return to Paul did not relieve Paul's anxieties regarding the Corinthians, for this had to await the meeting with Titus (II Cor. 2:13; 7:5-7), and this could mean that Timothy himself had not fared well at their hands. Now that the situation was much improved, the mention of Timothy may have been a thoughtful gesture by the author to reestablish Timothy's importance as a valued colaborer in apostolic ministries. This faithful brother is mentioned in ten of Paul's epistles (plus Hebrews), and appears in the opening greeting of six of them. Two of Paul's letters were addressed to him.

B. The Addressees (1:1b)

1. The church at Corinth

This congregation, located in the important commercial center at Corinth, had been founded during Paul's second missionary journey (Acts 18). The city, comprised of well over a half-million inhabitants at the time, was located on the isthmus connecting Peloponnesus with the rest of Greece. It was at the spot where shipping from the Aegean Sea and the

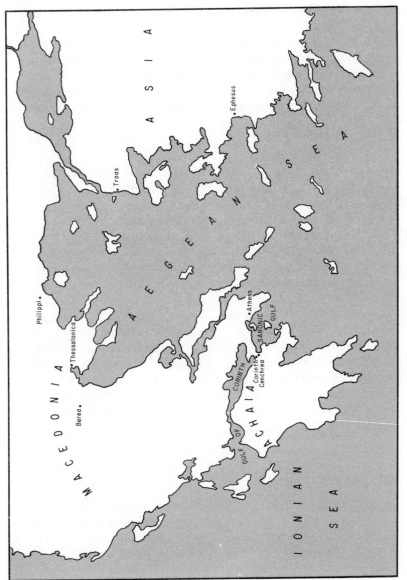

Fig. 2   Map of ancient Greece.

Saronic Gulf was often transferred overland to other vessels at the Gulf of Corinth and the Ionian Sea (see Fig. 2). In this bustling center of business, a church had been established. It was an active, thriving church, but one with diverse problems—a circumstance not surprising when its cosmopolitan setting is considered. (See I Corinthians for an overview of the church's problems.)

Paul had spent eighteen months in Corinth, preaching whenever possible and supporting himself by tentmaking (Acts 18:1-17). He previously had written the Corinthians at least two letters and probably a third one before he wrote II Corinthians. He also may have made a second visit to them and was now contemplating a third (see Introduction, "Background of II Corinthians").

2. The saints throughout Achaia

Achaia was the Roman province of which Corinth was the capital. It consisted of all the territory of Greece south of Macedonia. "Saints" (from *hagioi,* "holy, sacred, dedicated to God") is another name for Christians or believers, who are so called because they have been set apart to God by the Holy Spirit from the sinful world system which had once claimed them. This epistle was sent to Corinth, but the apostle knew it would be circulated among other churches in the area. How many Achaian churches existed at this time is not known, but we do know of a church at Cenchrea (Rom. 16:1) as well as at Corinth, and of Christians at Athens (Acts 17:34).

C. The Salutation (1:2)

VERSE 2. The familiar Pauline greeting, "Grace to you and peace from God our Father and the Lord Jesus Christ," is the same as that found in Romans, I Corinthians, Galatians, Ephesians, Philippians, II Thessalonians, and Philemon, and is similar to salutations in his other epistles. The twin blessings of grace and peace are a joining of common Greek and Hebrew salutations, with a Christian modification to fit Paul's purpose.[1] No

---

1. Letters in Greek usually began with *chairein* ("greetings," Acts 15:23; James 1:1), which Paul regularly transformed to *charis* ("grace"). The common Hebrew salutation was *šalōm* ("peace").

mere formality was this greeting. Rather, it sought for his readers the unmerited favor of God to sustain them in every circumstance, together with that inner and outward peace that transcends all turmoil because it comes from God who is our loving Father and Jesus Christ who is our guiding Lord.

D. The Thanksgiving (1:3-7)

1. For God's comfort in suffering (1:3-7)

VERSE 3. Because Paul had been under severe strain in recent weeks, due in no small part to his concern for the Corinthians (2:4, 12-13; 7:5), he was especially mindful of how God had been ministering to him in tenderness and encouragement. Therefore he shared with his readers his thanks to God, and reminded them that they too were beneficiaries of God's gracious ministration.

The object of Paul's thanksgiving was God, who is described by three significant phrases. First, He is designated as "the God and Father of our Lord Jesus Christ." For the Christian this is the most meaningful of identifications, for Jesus became the revealer of God to men in the clearest and most personal way (John 1:18; 14:9). This designation reminds us of the two modes of existence which Christ had. In His eternal being, God was always His Father; in His incarnation as the Messiah, God was His God, as Jesus Himself said on various occasions (Matt. 27:46; John 20:17).

God is also characterized as "the Father of mercies." This concept was rooted in Old Testament revelation, and found frequent expression among those who trusted God (II Sam. 24:14; I Chron. 21:13; Neh. 9:31; Ps. 51:1; 103:4; Isa. 54:7; Dan. 9:9). In His capacity as Father, He is the highest source of those tender compassions which the distressed and suffering require. Finally, He is called "the God of all comfort." This expression focuses attention on God's compassions as put into operation. Such English words as "encouragement," "help," and "advocacy" convey part of the rich meaning of this term. One has the impression that Paul's words were colored by recent personal experience.

VERSE 4. The words "us" and "we" appear frequently in this passage. It is clear from the contrasting use of "your" (v. 6) that Paul was not speaking generally of all men or all Christians when he said "us," but of himself and his associates. He meant that he and Timothy had been the beneficiaries of God's effective comfort, and that he viewed this blessing as not merely theirs alone but possessed of a wider purpose. They had suffered and were divinely comforted and encouraged so that they might more effectively encourage others who needed comfort. What an exalted way to regard one's afflictions—not merely as an instrument to teach him a lesson, but as a means to equip him to comfort others.

VERSE 5. Paul was no stranger to the need for comfort. He had experienced "the sufferings of Christ" in abundance. By this expression he referred not to Christ's agony on the cross as the substitute for our sin (those sufferings could not be shared with others), but to the various afflictions which Christ endured from a sinful world and which His followers also incur. Our Lord Himself predicted such suffering for those who would follow Him (Luke 14:27; John 15:18-20; 16:2-3, 33), and Paul accepted this fact as a part of his duty (Col. 1:24).

The apostle had discovered, however, that God's comfort through Christ was as abundant as the suffering. "Just as (*kathōs*) . . . so (*houtōs*)" expresses a comparison in which the second element matches the first. Although the sufferings seem to overflow (*perisseuei*), the encouragement and comfort for enduring the trial is just as abundant if only we would be spiritually sensitive enough to recognize it.

VERSE 6. Resuming the thought that his experience had a beneficial result for the Corinthians, Paul stated that in those cases when he was afflicted[2] the purpose was to assist the Corinthians in their daily walk in salvation. And in those times when God's comfort was being ministered to him, the divine purpose was that the Corinthians might also be comforted and encouraged when they learned it. The example of God's gracious dealings with Paul would have the effect of strengthening the Corinthians' endurance as they went through similar sufferings for their faith.

---

2. A form of conditional statement is used in which the indicative mood implies that an actual experience, not just a possible one, is assumed, at least for the moment.

VERSE 7. Paul concluded this thought by stating his confidence that the Corinthians were sharers of the same comfort from God as was Paul, even as they had shared his sufferings. The previous unpleasantness which had marked his relations with the church at Corinth had not soured his attitude toward its members nor caused him to despair of their commitment to Christ. He and Timothy knew[3] that whatever sufferings for Christ the church there had incurred, the Corinthian Christians had found the gracious comfort of God to be sufficient. The specific sufferings experienced by these Christians are not enumerated, but there are implications in Acts of various hostile groups in Corinth that could have incited persecution after Paul's visit (Acts 18:6, 10).

2. For God's deliverance of Paul in Asia (1:8-11)

VERSE 8. The second aspect of Paul's thanksgiving dealt with a specific instance of affliction and God's deliverance of him and Timothy in Asia. (The previous paragraph had discussed more generally "all our troubles" and "any trouble." See 1:4, NIV.) Asia was the Roman province on the west coast of Asia Minor. Its capital was Ephesus, where Paul had spent nearly three years (Acts 19:8, 10; 20:31). During the time in Ephesus Paul had been endangered by the riot of the silversmiths, although this was after Timothy had left (Acts 19:22). What other trials may have come to the missionaries in Ephesus before the riot are not reported by Luke in Acts. Perhaps the mention of "Asia" rather than Ephesus implies that the experience referred to occurred after Paul had left the capital city and was elsewhere in the province en route to Macedonia (Acts 20:1). By this time Timothy had returned with news from Corinth, and the two of them could have undergone the frightening experience mentioned here. It was so serious that life itself was threatened and death seemed inescapable.

VERSE 9. The expression "sentence of death" utilizes a rare word, *apokrima,* occurring nowhere else in biblical literature. The word is now known to be a technical term denoting an official resolution which decides

---

3. The participle "knowing" (*eidotes*) is used somewhat irregularly, having no expressed nominative on which it depends. However, the sense is clear that Paul means "we" are the ones "knowing" (from the use of *hēmōn* in the context). See 7:5 and 9:11 for other examples in this epistle.

a matter.[4] Whatever the circumstance was, it was so dire that Paul and Timothy felt as if an official death sentence had been passed on them. The use of the perfect tense "have had" (*eschēkamen*) implies that the condition continued to exist. Inasmuch as Timothy and Paul were still free men able to travel, the reference here must be metaphorical rather than an actual legal pronouncement. Furthermore, the resolution was "within ourselves," that is, an inner conviction rather than a verdict levied on them by others. Nevertheless it was a genuine understanding that their situation looked humanly hopeless. Their only hope was to trust in God who not only can rescue from the prospect of certain death, but even raise the dead if it is His will. This example of Paul and Timothy should encourage every reader to find the spiritual goals that can be pursued even in the most painful and discouraging circumstances.

VERSE 10. Paul's and Timothy's trust in God did not go unrewarded. God did rescue them out of their deadly peril. Paul was so thrilled with God's deliverance that he used the verb three times in this verse. A variation in the tense of the second use occurs among the manuscripts. The KJV follows manuscripts which give the three verbs as past (aorist), present, and future: "delivered . . . doth deliver . . . will yet deliver." The NASB and NIV follow older manuscripts[5] which have the second and third verbs as future. The sense, however, is essentially the same: God had delivered them in the recent past from this frightening trial; He will deliver them in the present and the immediate future; and He will still deliver them in years to come.

VERSE 11. The thought is concluded by Paul's warm and gracious assumption that the Corinthians would be joining together with each other and with the missionaries in expressing this need for continuing deliverance. Paul viewed the expected answer as a gracious favor given to himself and Timothy (*to eis hēmas charisma*), and regarded it as resulting from the prayers of many. Although Paul's trust was clearly in God and not in men (vv. 9-10), he also recognized that God has chosen to accomplish many of His plans by utilizing His people's actions, one of which is prayer.

4. Friedrich Büchsel, "Apokrima," TDNT, III, 945-946.
5. P⁴⁶ Aleph B C P.

When God has answered these concerted prayers, thanksgiving can then be offered as praise to God from a multitude of grateful people. If the expression "many persons" (KJV, NASB) is given its more usual translation, "many faces" (*pollōn prosōpōn*), it is suggestive of the upturned faces of these thankful petitioners.[6]

Many interpreters understand the peril that Paul mentioned as some serious illness of the apostle, perhaps his "thorn in the flesh" (12:7). This explanation fits well, provided that one is prepared to accept that the "we" and "us" in the passage refer only to Paul. However, the use of "I" in verse 15 and elsewhere argues against explaining the plurals as Paul's avoidance of the singular in personal references for reasons of modesty. Furthermore, the mention of deliverance in 1:10 is similar to Paul's descriptions of persecution rather than references to illness in other passages (Rom. 15:31; II Tim. 4:17-18). It is wiser to regard Paul's plural pronouns as genuine plurals unless the context will not permit it.

In this beautiful introduction Paul found occasion to be thankful in the most trying circumstances. Even suffering has benefits. It provides the occasion to experience God's comfort, to watch Him answer prayer, and to observe how believers can be strengthened in their Christian walk and witness by another's circumstances.

Questions for Discussion

1. What are some characteristics of II Corinthians which distinguish it from other epistles of Paul?
2. What are some of the reasons why God comforts His suffering children?
3. Describe an instance in which your suffering enabled you to help someone else.
4. What lessons have you learned from suffering? What have you learned that was similar to Paul's experience?
5. How do the prayers of Christians help in bringing God's deliverance to the afflicted?

---

6. Even though no other clear New Testament usage occurs, no serious objection exists to the translation "persons," for *prosōpon* has this meaning in nonbiblical Greek.

PAUL'S RELATIONS
WITH THE CORINTHIANS
(II Corinthians 1:12—7:16)

2

When Plans Must Change

II Corinthians 1:12—2:13

Giving up one's plans is not always easy. The more forethought and care that go into the planning, the more difficult it often is to accept alteration. If one has made his schedule carefully, and presumably has been sensitive to the will of God, factors which would force changes may be viewed by others with suspicion.

A complicating feature occurs when Christians hold conflicting views of the will of God. Paul faced this problem in his ministry. On several occasions he was convinced that God was leading him in a certain course of action, but his Christian friends were equally convinced that God's will lay in a different direction (Acts 20:22-24; cf. Acts 21:4, 11-14).

The following passage in II Corinthians is a reminder that God frequently leads one step at a time. Long-range plans may need to be modified as time goes by. In Paul's case, his original plans were made in good faith with the best information he had at the time. Circumstances had altered, however, and it was necessary to revise those plans. Certain features had come into clearer focus, and sensitivity to God's will for the next step required some changes. The possibility that some of his Christian readers might misunderstand and question the reasons for change prompted this portion of the letter.

II. Paul's Relations with the Corinthians (1:12—7:16)

A. *The Change of Itinerary (1:12—2:13)*

1. The original plan (1:12-22)

   a. *The plan was formed in sincerity (1:12-14)*

VERSE 12. Our versions vary in their translation of *kauchēsis,* using such renderings as "rejoicing" (KJV), "proud confidence" (NASB), and "boast" (NIV). The term emphasizes the action rather than the content, so the thought is, "Our act of boasting should be understood in this way." Paul meant that when he and Timothy engaged in justifiable glorying regarding what God had been accomplishing through them, it followed the pattern which he next explained. Boasting is unseemly when it is mere bragging about one's own accomplishments. But the term (*kauchēsis*) is often used in Scripture to describe a proper testifying of the trustworthiness of God (e.g., Ps. 32:11).[1]

These faithful men could glory as they did because it was the testimony of their consciences that God had approved their conduct. The conscience is one's inner consciousness regarding the rightness of his actions. When Christians are enlightened by the Word of God and the Holy Spirit, and then walk in full harmony with that knowledge, their consciences will approve their actions. Paul and Timothy were convinced that their ministry in general and their dealings with the Corinthians in particular had been performed in "holiness[2] and sincerity that are from God" (NIV), and their

---

1. LXX, Psalm 31:11.

2. Although the reading *hagiotēti* ("holiness") is supported by such ancient witnesses as P[46] Aleph A B C K P, and is adopted by NASB and NIV, the alternative *haplotēti* ("simplicity") found in Western and Byzantine sources is adopted by all three United Bible Societies (UBS) editions (with a "D" rating indicative of a high degree of doubt). The latter reading is used in KJV. Bruce M. Metzger lists three reasons for the editors' choice: 1) context favors "simplicity" rather than "holiness"; 2) *haplotēs* occurs frequently in II Cor.; 3) *hagiotēs* never is used elsewhere by Paul. *A Textual Commentary on the Greek New Testament,* p. 575.

consciences supported that assertion. They made no claim to a superiority of inherent personal fitness ("fleshly wisdom"), but gave all credit to "the grace of God." Hence their boasting could not be attributed to human pride, but to an eagerness to exult in what God had done.

VERSE 13. Paul seemed to be responding to certain criticisms in this section of the letter. Apparently his detractors at Corinth were accusing him of unreliability or deviousness. He was alleged to be without integrity, insincere, and one whose writings could not be totally believed. On the contrary, insisted Paul, there was no need to read between the lines of his letters, for everything he had meant to convey was clearly expressed in his previous letters (of which there were at least two and probably three).[3] These were in the Corinthians' possession, and they were reading those letters and understanding them. If certain changes had been made in Paul's plans, the reasons were to be found in more recent circumstances, not in subterfuge or unreliability on the part of Paul and those with him ("we").

It is possible to punctuate the last part of verse 13 as the beginning of a new sentence, and the thought is considerably clearer when this is done: "I hope you will continue to understand until the end . . ." (NIV). The next verse completes the thought and makes clear "the end" Paul had in mind.

VERSE 14. The clause, "just as you also partially did understand us," points to the fact that some of the Corinthians did recognize Paul's integrity and did not join the ranks of his accusers. These stalwart supporters of the apostle had understood his forthrightness and his purposes, and he longed for that trust to continue. He desired that they be confirmed in their understanding so that they could boast about him just as he expected to do regarding them "in the day of the Lord Jesus" (KJV, NIV).[4]

---

3. The "lost letter," I Corinthians, and the "severe letter" (see Introduction).

4. An expression occurring with only slight variation six times in the New Testament, three of them in the Corinthian epistles (I Cor. 1:8; 5:5; II Cor. 1:14; Phil. 1:6, 10; 2:16). It is similar to the "day of the Lord" (I Thess. 5:2) and the Old Testament "day of Jehovah" (Amos

This identifies "the end" (*heōs telous*) mentioned in verse 13. When we stand before Christ and give account of our deeds at His tribunal (5:10) all issues will be made plain. At that time Paul expects the presence of the Corinthian believers to provide him with abundant cause for glorying, for they were the fruit of his labors. Likewise the loyal Corinthians who had come to know him fully had found him to be a real cause for glorying, for he had labored faithfully among them and even now was deeply involved in promoting their welfare.

b. The plan involved two visits to Corinth (1:15-22)

VERSE 15. With the confidence that the Corinthians were as fully appreciative of him as he was of them (v. 14), Paul had planned to visit them and presumably had communicated this information to them. Difficulties in translation[5] and somewhat confusing data pose problems for the interpreter. The matter is complicated by the mention of an itinerary in I Corinthians 16:5 which differs from the one referred to here. It seems unlikely that the reference in this verse to a second visit which had to be cancelled referred to Paul's next contemplated trip, for he had already been in Corinth twice by the time of this writing, and his next visit would be his third (12:14; 13:1). It is better, therefore, to understand Paul to mean that he had planned to come to Corinth first before proceeding to Macedonia. The "second benefit" (KJV) or "twice receive a blessing" (NASB) is explained in the following verse as resulting from a double visit. The manuscripts vary between *charin* ("grace, favor, benefit") and *charan* ("joy"). Both fit the context easily, but most translators and interpreters have preferred *charin* as more characteristic of Paul.

5:18-20), although without the emphasis on punishment. It refers to the time of Christ's return for His church and the examination of believers' works.

5. The interpreter must decide whether *proteron* should be rendered "originally" or "formerly," and construed with "intended," or translated "first" and related to the infinitive "to come to you first." He must also decide between the variants *charis* ("grace, favor, benefit") or *chara* ("joy"), both of which have early support.

VERSE 16. The precise itinerary (as originally planned) called for a sea voyage from Ephesus to Corinth, then a land journey to Macedonia, a second visit to Corinth on the return, and finally a trip to Judea with the assistance[6] of the Corinthians (see map, Fig. 2). When Paul had written I Corinthians, he had given a different route, planning to come to Corinth by way of Macedonia (16:5). Obviously one of those plans had changed, for he was already in Macedonia and planning to visit Corinth afterward (9:2-4). Even assuming the accomplishment of the painful visit (see Introduction, "Background'), certain features of the plan as first announced (I Cor. 16:5) had been altered, and this had led to charges of vacillation. Yet the unpleasantness that had erupted had ruined the prospect of that dual blessing from a two-phase visit.

VERSE 17. Knowing what some people at Corinth were saying about these changes in plans, Paul asked, "When I was planning this, I didn't use lightness, did I?" (literal). The answer he expected to such a question was no. Men of good will should recognize that his plans had not been made lightly but honestly, with their interests at heart. The second question, translated literally, looked at his present planning: "Or what I am presently planning, am I planning according to the flesh, so that with me it is 'Yes, yes' and 'No, no' [that is, at the same time]?" There is a strong likelihood that Paul was actually quoting some of the phrases used against him. The articles with "lightness," "yes, yes," and "no, no" can be understood as "the lightness of which I am accused," and "the contradictory yesses and nos which you fault me for." These rhetorical questions imply that his ministry was not carried out according to mere human whim ("the flesh").

VERSE 18. Paul reminded his readers that God's character is completely trustworthy, and one may expect His apostolic messengers to be the same. The Corinthians had every reason to believe that Paul and his companions had always spoken truth to them, for Paul's message had been the Word of God. To question Paul's veracity was to cast reflection on the One who gave

6. The verb *propempō* ("send forward") can mean "to accompany or escort" (Acts 20:38; 21:5), or "to help on one's journey" by supplying food, money, or companions (Acts 15:3; I Cor. 16:6). Arndt, p. 716.

him his message and directed his movements. To imply that Paul's character was unreliable on the basis of a schedule which was altered (for valid reasons that will be explained later) was unwarranted and probably malicious.

VERSE 19. In demonstrating his own trustworthiness, Paul aligned himself with "the Son of God, Jesus Christ, who was preached among you by us" (KJV). What the Corinthians knew of Christ they had learned from Paul, and it certainly would be strange to accept Christ as worthy of their trust on the basis of a proclamation by untrustworthy preachers! How could the Corinthianss be confident that they had been told the truth? "Us" is here shown to be a true plural, referring to Paul, Silvanus (often called Silas), and Timothy. These three had labored together during the founding of the church at Corinth (Acts 18:5), and their testimony had been consistent. It was not vacillating, tentative, or questionable. It had been a clear affirmation ("yes") of God's truth as centered in Christ. Would the church accept their preaching of Christ, and then reject the preachers themselves as untrustworthy? The inconsistency would appear to rest with the detractors at Corinth, not with Paul and his companions.

VERSE 20. All of the promises of God, as a matter of fact, are made possible to men because of Christ and His ministry. It is because believers have been born again through their relationship with Him that they have come to understand God's truth, and can add their "Amen" to express their assent to what God has revealed. The article with "Amen" (*to amēn*) suggests Paul's reference as being to the customary amen, the early liturgical practice of using "amen" at the conclusion of prayers or in response to a reading of the Word of God. This practice was well established in Old Testament times (Deut. 27:15-26). The early church continued the use of the expression to denote agreement (I Cor. 14:16; Rev. 22:20). The term also was a title given to Christ, as the faithful and true witness to divine truth (Rev. 3:14). The thought is rounded out by the reminder that our "amen" brings glory to God because the promises of God to which it assents have their validity through Christ (*di' autou*).

VERSE 21. As Paul concluded this explanation of his original plan to visit the Corinthians twice, he climaxed his answer to the charge of fickleness by a reminder of what God has done in the lives of all Christians. Any action that deliberately drives a wedge of conflict between God's people has failed to recognize what God is accomplishing in them.

The subject of verse 21 is God. Four of His actions toward believers are mentioned. First, He is the one who "establishes us with you in Christ." It is God who continually[7] acts in maintaining the union of all believers in Christ, so that their faith may grow more firm. Inasmuch as this was true of Paul, Silas, and Timothy, and of the Corinthians, any efforts to disrupt this unity would be at cross-purposes with God's present action.

Second, God has anointed all believers ("us" here includes both "us" and "you" of the previous phrase). This act and the next two are past actions of God, occurring at the conversion of each believer. The meaning of "Christ" is "Anointed One," and the concept involves God's bestowing of the Spirit on the Messiah to grant Him this position and to empower Him for the task (Isa. 61:1-3; Luke 4:18). Believers have been joined in vital union with Christ, and have been anointed by God also (I John 2:20). It is clear from other passages that the Holy Spirit Himself is the anointing for believers (I John 2:27), just as He was for Christ. This occurs for each believer at conversion.

VERSE 22. Third, God has sealed believers. The ancient seal was an impress on wax or clay that denoted ownership (the owner's identity was engraved on the seal) and security (an unbroken seal meant the contents were undisturbed). This sealing also was provided by the gift of the Holy Spirit to believers, marking them as God's own (Eph. 1:13; II Tim. 2:19) and protecting them until the final phase of redemption (Eph. 4:30).

Fourth, God has given the Holy Spirit as the pledge that all His redemptive promises will be fulfilled. The *arrabōn* was a deposit or earnest money which gave legal claim to some contract.[8] By bestowing the Spirit on each believer, God has guaranteed the successful outcome of salvation in all of its issues. What we now enjoy in the way of spiritual life and enlightenment is just a foretaste of what is yet to come.

---

7. *bebaiōn* is a present participle, "continually engaged in establishing or making firm."

8. Johannes Behm, "Arrabon," TDNT, I, 475.

The Triune God had thus been involved by Paul in pointing his readers to the grandeur of salvation. One should reflect soberly on what God has done for believers before he embarks on a course which would tear apart the unity which God is forming.

2. Postponement of the plan (1:23—2:4)

VERSE 23. "I call God as my witness" (NIV). This solemn assertion emphasizes Paul's desire to be regarded as absolutely truthful. Although some commentators call this an oath,[9] there is no reason why it cannot be viewed merely as a statement that God knew full well the truthfulness of Paul's testimony.[10]

Paul explained that the changing of the original plan was because of his desire to spare the Corinthians further sorrow. He knew from the previous "painful visit" (2:1) that their problems were not over, and that if he had come as first planned he would need to deal severely with certain offenses. The delay, then, was to avoid an unpleasant confrontation.

VERSE 24. With great sensitivity, however, Paul realized that even this mention of sparing might be misunderstood by some of the Corinthians. They might interpret it as an implication that Paul would have exercised autocratic power if he had come. Not so, said Paul. Neither he nor his associates ("we") ever did this. On the contrary, they regarded themselves as coworkers (*sunergoi*) with the Corinthians to develop their spiritual joy,[11] rather than to provoke the sorrow that a nonsparing visit would have caused. Also, Paul always understood and taught that it was "by faith" (*tēi pistei*)[12] that believers have their standing in Christ, not by complying with

9. See Alfred Plummer, *Corinthians Two,* in the International Critical Commentary series, pp. 42-43; Philip E., Hughes, *Commentary on the Second Epistle to the Corinthians,* in the New International Commentary series, pp. 46-47.

10. This avoids the problem of oath-taking in the light of the New Testament injunctions against it (Matt. 5:33-37; James 5:12).

11. "Your joy" (*tēs charas humōn*) is an objective genitive.

12. Although the dative could be regarded as indicating reference, "in regard to the faith," the similarity to Romans 11:20 makes it more likely an instrumental use (KJV, NIV).

the demands of human lords. Each person is on his own before God (Rom. 14:4).

VERSE 1. Inasmuch as 1:24 was something of a digression, 2:1 resumes the thought of 1:23. Paul had decided to postpone a trip to Corinth because he did not wish to cause further pain, either to the Corinthians or to himself. The implication is that a previous visit had been a painful one, and he had determined "not again in pain to come" (literal). This could not have been a reference to his first visit (Acts 18), and must therefore imply that a subsequent visit had occurred prior to this letter. This is corroborated in 13:1, where the apostle's proposed visit is called his third one (see Introduction, "Background"). Although some scholars think the unrecorded painful visit occurred prior to the time Paul wrote I Corinthians,[13] absence of any reference to it in that epistle makes it more likely that it occurred during the interval between the writing of the two canonical epistles.[14]

VERSE 2. Paul hastened to make it clear that he received no joy from causing pain to the Corinthians. On the contrary, it was the Corinthians to whom he looked for joy. How could he expect to find joy from those whom he had just put to grief? It was to Paul's advantage to provide the Corinthians with reasons for rejoicing, as long as truth and godly conduct were not compromised. Causing pain to the Corinthians would bring pain to Paul, too.

VERSE 3. Consequently, instead of making still another painful visit, Paul had chosen the alternative of writing "this . . . very thing." Some scholars regard the previous letter as I Corinthians,[15] although the description of it in the next verse is hardly characteristic of that epistle as a whole. It appears more likely that the reference is to a letter no longer extant, to be designated henceforth as the severe letter (see Introduction, "Back-

13. Paul's painful visit is placed prior to I Corinthians by R. C. H. Lenski, *Interpretation of First and Second Corinthians,* p. 866, and Philip E. Hughes, *Commentary,* p. 52.

14. The painful visit is placed after I Corinthians by C. K. Barrett, *The Second Epistle to the Corinthians,* pp. 85-86, and Murray J. Harris, "2 Corinthians," *The Expositor's Bible Commentary,* X, 302.

15. Hughes, *Commentary,* pp. 54-58.

ground"). Paul had sent it in order to avoid another painful confrontation in person. He was confident that when the issues causing all the trouble at Corinth were finally rectified, the result would be joy in the church and for himself as well.

VERSE 4. The severe letter, written out of a heart torn with anguished concern, had not been intended to inflict pain and grief on the Corinthians, although this presumably would have occurred. Paul's only purpose in using such strong means was to rectify an unfortunate situation for the Corinthians' ultimate good. He was not interested in using the lash except for the wholesome results he hoped it would bring. Specifically, he wanted his readers to be aware of the great love he had for them. They should recognize that his strong words brought him no pleasure; the only reason he went to this extreme and risked their displeasure was his desire to further their best interests. This love (*agapēn*) was not the love of sentimentality or mere emotion, but an earnest desire to provide what was best for them. "More abundantly" (KJV; *perissoterōs*) or "especially" (NASB) suggests that this whole business with the Corinthian church had claimed more of Paul's efforts than any other church up to this time. Surely the Corinthians should recognize what he had undergone for them and be understanding of his change in plans.

3. Forgiveness advised for the offender (2:5-11)

VERSE 5. Insufficient data prevent us from identifying the offender with any real assurance. The older commentators generally explained this passage in terms of the man involved in incest (I Cor. 5).[16] It is more common today, however, to view the case as involving someone who resisted Paul's authority on his painful visit.[17] Perhaps the opponent was one who objected to Paul's use of authority and may have denounced Paul's handling of the case of the incestuous man. Whatever the precise occasion,

16. For a recent discussion of this view by one who holds it, see Hughes, *Commentary*, pp. 59-65.

17. Plummer, *Corinthians Two*, pp. 54-55; Barrett, *Second Epistle*, p. 89; Harris, "2 Corinthians," pp. 328-329.

the offender appears to be one who had somehow opposed Paul and this had prompted Paul's severe letter (2:9).

Paul said that the anguish caused by the offender had not been experienced by the apostle so much as by the Corinthians themselves. At least it was true of most of them (*apo merous,* "from a part, in part"). Doubtless the offender had some supporters who were not grieved by his antagonism toward Paul, so the apostle was careful to qualify his all-inclusive statement (author's version, "that I may not exaggerate").[18]

VERSE 6. Nevertheless it was time to recognize that the congregational discipline which had been performed on this person who had done the wrong had been sufficient. Apparently it had not been a unanimous decision (rather, "by the majority"). Now was the moment for grace and forgiveness. To prolong the punishment would be unwise.

VERSE 7. To "forgive and comfort" is literally "to act graciously toward (*charisasthai*) and to encourage (*parakalesai*)." This admonition agrees with the teaching of Jesus, who said, "If your brother sins, rebuke him, and if he repents, forgive him" (Luke 17:3, NIV). Discipline which has its desired effect must be responded to with appropriate action. Vindictiveness and an unforgiving spirit are as sinful as the offender's deed (Matt. 18:21-35).

The reason Paul gave for urging the display of forgiveness by the Corinthians was not their personal obligation before God, but the ultimate well-being of the offender. To withhold forgiveness and restoration could cause such excessive remorse as to bring utter despair and even abandonment of the faith. The word "swallowed up" (KJV) or "overwhelmed" (NASB, NIV) was used of a lion devouring its prey (I Peter 5:8), of Egyptians drowned in the sea (Heb. 11:29), and of death being completely done away by resurrection (I Cor. 15:54). Paul regarded a grieving penitent still under discipline as being in similar straits.

18. Another view of the clause *hina mē epibarō* regards the meaning as "that I may not overburden [the offender with too much blame]." See H. A. W. Meyer, *Critical and Exegetical Handbook to the Epistles to the Corinthians,* in the Commentary on the New Testament series (Winona Lake, IN: BMH Books, reprinted 1979), VI, pp. 443-445; Hughes, *Commentary,* p. 65, note.

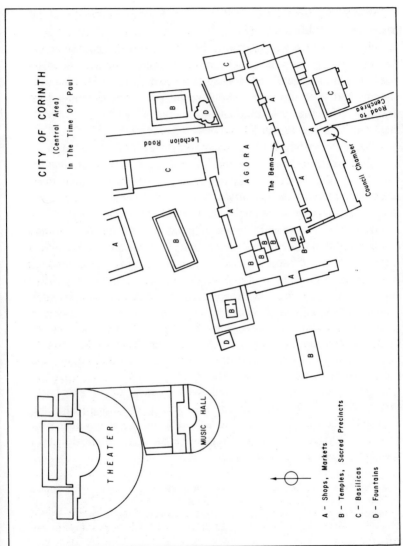

Fig. 3 City of Corinth (central area) in the time of Paul.

VERSE 8. This being the case, Paul encouraged the church to "confirm" (KJV; "reaffirm," NASB, NIV) its love to the party who had been punished. The church members were to make it clear to this man that his restoration was genuine and heartfelt. Whether this implies some formal act of ratification is not certain. The important thing was that personal actions by the members should be forthcoming, proving to the offender beyond any doubt that genuine love existed for him.

VERSE 9. When Paul said he "wrote" (*egrapsa*) for this reason, he probably was referring to the previous severe letter (2:3), which no longer exists. He had written the severe letter to set forth the course of action the Corinthians should take in dealing with their problem. Their reaction would reveal the level of their willingness to obey the apostle's authority. Would they follow his instruction only in exercising discipline against sinning members? Or would they be equally observant in following through with forgiveness at the proper time? Human justice is not always performed with evenhandedness. Even judges trained in the law and the judicial system do not always make the punishment fit the crime. Small wonder that ordinary people, including members of Christian churches, can be easily confused in determining the time when punishment is sufficient and restoration is in order.

VERSE 10. The apostle wanted his readers to know that he would fully concur with their decision to forgive the offender in their problem case. Paul was already aware that the Corinthians had changed their attitude and were now warmly supportive of the apostle (7:6-7). He informed them that he would also forgive anyone they would forgive (and perhaps had already forgiven).

Paul further told the Corinthians that his forgiveness of the offender was actually done for their sakes, and the next verse will explain why this was so. "If I forgave any thing" (KJV) is a parenthetical statement, implying either that Paul had already forgiven any personal insults, perhaps during his painful visit (2:4), or else was his modest assertion that he could easily put aside such attacks against himself. The statement also suggests that the problem was more likely a case of personal insult against the apostle, to which he could graciously and modestly respond, rather than the case of incest (I Cor. 5) where these words would be most unlikely.

VERSE 11. The reason why Paul wanted the offender restored, and had taken certain preliminary steps himself (such as granting his personal forgiveness), was to deny Satan the opportunity of outwitting the Corinthians and exploiting the situation. If the object of Paul's previous severity were not fully restored after his repentance, Satan might use the occasion to divide the church, as well as to demoralize permanently the man himself. "We" and "us" in this verse refer to Paul and the Corinthian congregation. Paul's experience with satanic exploitation had doubtless been shared with his various congregations. His clear understanding of the potential hazards in this case was revealed by the advice he gave, and made it clear that Satan's schemes were no secret to him and should not be to his readers.

4. Adoption of a revised plan (2:12-13)

VERSE 12. Instead of following the original plan mentioned in 1:16, Paul had decided to travel through Macedonia first. Leaving Ephesus (Acts 20:1), he went to Troas, either by land or on a coasting vessel. Troas was a port on the Aegean coast of western Asia Minor at the mouth of the Dardanelles (see map, Fig. 2). The city was founded in 300 B.C. (Homeric Troy is about 10 miles away). Its full name was Alexandria Troas. It was Asia's nearest port to Europe and thus of considerable importance. From here Paul first went to Europe on his second missionary journey (Acts 16:8-11). No mention occurs in Acts of any church being founded at that time. It is more likely that the church was founded on the occasion described in this letter to the Corinthians. Some months later Paul would revisit Troas and meet with the church at its regular gathering on the first day of the week (Acts 20:6-12).

Paul had come to Troas to proclaim the gospel of Christ. The exact length of his stay is not indicated. It must have been long enough for a church to be established, and also for him to see that a wide-open ministry lay before him if he should feel free to take it. He had previously written the Corinthians that a wide door for effective service was open to him at Ephesus (I Cor. 16:8-9). Now in Troas the same situation existed. The opportunity for serving the Lord was clearly open.

VERSE 13. Nevertheless Paul had no peace in his heart to remain at Troas further. The expression "no rest for my spirit" is similar to his later description of this same episode, "our flesh had no rest" (7:5). In both instances he meant that he was too restless to remain in spite of the great opportunity at Troas.

The reason for this restlessness was that Titus had not arrived at Troas. Apparently Titus was the associate who had been sent to Corinth with the severe letter, and Paul had hoped for an early return with good news from the church. Presumably Paul and Titus had planned to meet at Troas. (For additional discussion of this matter, see 7:5-16.)

Titus is mentioned in II Corinthians, Galatians, II Timothy, and Titus. He was a Gentile who accompanied Paul and Barnabas on an early trip to Jerusalem (Gal. 2:1-3). He next appears in the record in connection with the church at Corinth, where he was sent by Paul to help resolve the difficulties there. He also made another visit to Corinth to assist in the collection for the Jerusalem Christians (II Cor. 8:16-24; 12:18). At a later time he carried out ministries in Crete (Titus 1:4-5) and Dalmatia (II Tim. 4:10) under Paul's direction.

Paul could wait for Titus no longer. His restless spirit drove him to Macedonia, with the plan of encountering Titus on the way. His chief reason for wanting to find Titus was to hear recent news from Corinth. Not even the open door at Troas could entice Paul from his deep desire to meet the needs at Corinth. Surely there was no basis for suspecting his motives or his love for the Corinthians.

Questions for Discussion

1. What principles do you see in this passage regarding the church's treatment of wrongdoers?
2. Why should Christians forgive one another?
3. What keeps some Christians from being as quick to forgive as they are to punish?
4. Why do Christians sometimes abandon godly leaders?
5. How should one decide between several attractive opportunities to serve the Lord?

3

The Glory of Christian Ministry

II Corinthians 2:14—3:18

Some activities have a special appeal about them. People are drawn to certain pursuits because of the excitement generated by the activity itself. Others are attracted by the financial rewards, by the adulation of an audience, or by the popular esteem in which some activities are held. The sense of satisfaction and fulfillment afforded by such occupations as medicine, education, and social work can lead to a career.

The Christian ministry was once one of those highly respected vocations. Shifting attitudes in recent years, however, have caused changes in society's values. Our scientific age tends to place on the pedestal of public esteem the research scientist, the surgeon, and the sports hero. Yet the reasons why the Christian minister once headed the list of respected leaders in American life are still valid and worthy of serious reflection.

The apostle Paul wrote in this passage about the activity that had captivated him. He was not attracted by any financial rewards, for it offered none to him. He gained from it no earthly pomp, no public prestige (except the respect of the Christians he had helped, and even this was mixed). He experienced abandonment and hatred from former friends, continual threats to his life, and hardships that would demoralize most men. Nevertheless he was so enthralled with the privilege of Christian ministry that he made it his career, and never found anything that could entice him away from this glorious passion of his life.

Although "the Christian ministry" is an expression often used to designate a certain career, "Christian ministry" should be an activity in which every believer is engaged. Even if ministry is not one's career, each Christian can share many of the same satisfactions that Paul describes here. Every Christian can enjoy the glory of this ministry when he understands what Christian ministry involves.

B. The Character of Paul's Ministry (2:14—6:10)

1. Paul's ministry was a sincere proclamation of the knowledge of Christ (2:14-17)

VERSE 14. At this point in the letter, Paul interrupted the description of his search for Titus, not resuming it until 7:5. Nevertheless the content of this section is pertinent to the discussion, for it reveals Paul's attitude of confidence in God's leading, even in times of disappointment. There is no need to suspect several documents have been combined here.

Although he had been concerned at not finding Titus in Troas (2:12-13), Paul could still express thanks to God for His unfailing leadership. Disappointment over certain details and events did not cause the apostle to lose sight of the larger aspect of God's program. He was convinced that God was always leading him and his associates in the triumphant accomplishment of His glorious will. The metaphor is probably that of the Roman triumph, in which a conquering general and his victorious legions would parade in Rome, displaying some of their captives and other trophies of war. In this use of the figure Paul seems to be equating his missionary party with the victorious forces in the triumph, rather than with the captives who would soon be executed.[1]

As part of a Roman triumph, garlands of flowers along the route and the burning of incense and spices provided a fragrant aroma that was one of the characteristics of the parade. So Paul recognized that whether he and Titus

1. The only other New Testament use of the verb *thriambeuō* ("lead in triumph") may be understood in the same way (Col. 2:15). See Homer A. Kent, Jr., *Treasures of Wisdom,* pp. 88–89. Another view, however, treats the verb as "display" or "make known." See Rory B. Egan, "Lexical Evidence on Two Pauline Passages," pp. 34-62.

Fig. 4 A Roman triumph, commemorating the capture of Jerusalem by Titus, depicted on the Arch of Titus in Rome.

were at Troas, or Corinth, or somewhere else, and whether circumstances were pleasant or grim, God was using His messengers to disseminate the precious knowledge of Himself in the gospel of Christ.

VERSE 15. In verse 14 the fragrance referred to the gospel which was proclaimed by Paul and his associates. In verse 15 the preachers themselves are identified with the gospel they preach. They are called a "fragrance of Christ" because they are the deliverers of that gospel.

Paradoxically these messengers of the gospel were a harbinger of diametrically opposite results to two groups of people. "Those who are being saved" and "those who are perishing" describe the two kinds of responses to the preaching of the gospel. At the Roman triumph the aroma of the incense was a token of victory and honor for the conquering legions, but was a sign of sure execution to the captives in the parade.

VERSE 16. The previous statement is further explained by this verse. To unbelievers the preachers who announced the gospel were proclaiming a message of eternal doom which would eventually be experienced in the unbeliever's destruction (*ek thanatou eis thanaton,* "out of death unto death"). To those who responded in faith, the gospel preacher had brought a message which comes from Christ, the source of true life, and produces life eternal (*ek zōēs eis zōēn,* "out of life unto life").[2]

The rhetorical question, "And who is sufficient for these things?" (KJV) has been answered differently by readers. Some have suggested the answer is, "We apostles are sufficient," inasmuch as they did not peddle a false message (2:17—3:1).[3] Others regard the answer to be, "No one is, if he depends on his own resources" (3:4-6). The latter explanation is preferable and could be expanded as follows: Certainly the religious peddlers are not sufficient, for they depend on a personal sufficiency with selfish motivation. Only those who depend solely on God for His sufficiency can hope to bear this heavy responsibility (3:5).

VERSE 17. Paul and his companions were not like "so many" (NIV),[4] who were "peddling the word of God" like common hucksters. The Greek term occurs only here in the New Testament. It is derived from the term for "retailer" (*kapēlos*), and carried the suggestion of trickery, deceit, and falsehood. The verb meant "to sell at illegitimate profit, to misrepresent, to hawk."[5] The picture comes to mind of a huckster haggling over prices, and cheapening his goods when necessary to make a sale.

By contrast, Paul's proclamation of the gospel was done with complete sincerity. The term "sincerity" (*eilikrineia*) always denoted moral purity, and was apparently derived from the words for "sun" (*hēlios*) and "test" (*krinō*). Hence the sense is "tested by the light of the sun, spotless, pure."[6] From the subjective side of Paul's own mind, he had spoken with purity. Objectively the source of his commission was from God (*ek theou*). Further-

2. Another view of these two *ek . . . eis* phrases regards them as simply indicating continuous progression as in Romans 1:17 ("from glory to glory"). J. H. Bernard, "Second Corinthians," *Expositor's Greek Testament,* III, 51.

3. R. C. H. Lenski, *Interpretation of First and Second Corinthians,* p. 902.

4. Greek: *hoi polloi.* It is not always necessary to press this to its extreme sense of "the majority."

5. See Hans Windisch, "Kapēleuō," TDNT, III, 603-605.

6. Friedrich Büchsel, "Eilikrinēs, . . . ," TDNT, II, 397-398.

more, he and his companions had carried on their ministry "in the sight of God," that is, with full consciousness that they were responsible to Him and were being watched by Him. Finally, they had spoken "in Christ," being fully aware of their position as members of Christ's body, and drawing power from their vital union with Him. Such a ministry left little room for suspicion.

2. The ministry's best recommendation was the lives of the Corinthian converts (3:1-3)

VERSE 1. At this point Paul felt a bit of awkwardness over the possibility that his previous statement might have sounded self-serving. The use of "again" could imply certain prior claims about himself made in previous contacts with the Corinthians, or perhaps may reflect accusations made against him by the religious "peddlers" (2:17) who caused him trouble. Lest the wrong impression be left, he quickly added another question which should have shown how baseless such a suspicion was. Surely Paul did not need letters of recommendation at this point, either to the Corinthians (he had led many of them to Christ and had founded their church), or from them (as if he depended on them for acceptance elsewhere). Letters of recommendation were a common practice when persons were otherwise unknown. The Corinthian church had once received one regarding Apollos (Acts 18:27). Antioch had received one from Jerusalem about Silas and Judas (Acts 15:25-27). Paul himself had written many such commendations (e.g., Phoebe, Rom. 16:1-2; Timothy, I Cor. 16:10-11; Barnabas, Col. 4:10). If Paul recently had been disparaged on grounds that no one had recommended him, then let the Corinthians pause to remember a few things.

VERSE 2. The Corinthians themselves were Paul's letter of recommendation, far better than formal credentials. Furthermore, they had formed such an important part of his ministry that it could be said they were actually inscribed in the hearts of the missionary party. Hence Paul and his companions had the interests of the Corinthians close to their hearts wherever they went. This living proof of Paul's authority and effectiveness as a minister of Christ should have been obvious to all persons who would take the trouble to examine the transformed lives of the Corinthians.

VERSE 3. Actually, it had been made clear[7] that the Corinthians were Christ's letter. Paul and his helpers were more like amanuenses[8] whom Christ had used to communicate His message. Christ was the One who had wrought the change in the Corinthians' lives. Through His power they had become His letter to the world, displaying what the gospel could do. As such they were no mere document written with ink but had been acted on by the Holy Spirit in regeneration. Nor were they like the inanimate tablets of stone in the old covenant of law given to Moses. Rather Christ had written His message on tablets of human hearts. This concept was undoubtedly based on the Old Testament prophecy of the new covenant (Jer. 31:33; cf. Heb. 8:8-12). The new covenant mediated by Christ through the Spirit produced an inward change whereby God's Word was actually implanted in believers, not just externally imposed. This transforming work made the believers Paul's greatest recommendation.

3. Paul proclaimed the new covenant (3:4-18)

a. The source of Paul's competence (3:4-6)

VERSE 4. The confidence Paul had that Christ was speaking through him was no mere personal boasting. This confidence had not resulted from any self-satisfaction based on strenuous effort, skillful performance, or unusual human competence. It was rather a conviction supplied by Christ Himself, and was a confidence that would stand up before God.

VERSE 5. Here Paul answered the question he raised in 2:16. Whatever adequacy or sufficiency he and his companions possessed was not the product of their own ability or origination. He did not deny that a competent piece of work had been done in the Corinthians' midst, but he disclaimed all personal credit. Adequacy for the task had come from God.

VERSE 6. It was God who had made His ministers competent for their task. Their ministry was the proclamation of the new covenant. This

7. Greek: *phaneroumenoi.* The term denotes making something visible which is invisible.
8. An amanuensis was a stenographer or copyist who did the actual writing for an author.

covenant had been promised to Israel (Jer. 31:31-34) as a replacement for the old Mosaic covenant. This covenant was God's promise to deal in grace with His people by forgiving their sin and granting them new hearts. The covenant was validated by the death of Christ (Matt. 26:28). Although national Israel has not yet experienced the fulfillment of this covenant, the spiritual benefits of it are available to every believer through the gospel. It was as a proclaimer of this new covenant which offered regeneration to men that Paul was carrying out his ministry.

The new covenant is "not of the letter, but of the Spirit." We must not suppose that the common English contrast between "letter" and "spirit" as distinguishing "the letter of the law" from its underlying spiritual principles is meant. Paul certainly did not mean that the literal meaning of the Old Testament is harmful, and that only spiritual principles or allegorical interpretations are valid. On the contrary, he was contrasting the two covenants, as is clear from the context. By "letter" he meant the old Mosaic covenant which was a document externally imposed on its adherents. "Spirit" characterizes the new covenant which provides an internal change wrought by the Spirit of God (3:3).

The contrast between the two covenants is noted in their results. "The letter kills" clearly refers to the Mosaic covenant, as verse 7 indicates. It killed in the sense that it confronted man with God's righteous standard but left him condemned to death. The law could not of itself provide righteousness. Regeneration, however, is produced by the Spirit and provides life for everyone who by faith comes under the provisions of the new covenant. This is not to imply that no one in the Old Testament had spiritual life. What it does indicate is that life comes by the action of the Spirit, not by human ability to keep God's standards. Old Testament saints were saved by faith in the transforming power and grace of God, just as Christians are.

b. The great glory of the new covenant (3:7-11)

VERSE 7. As Paul continued to describe his ministry as involving the preaching of the new covenant, he showed its superiority over the old covenant. Doubtless the opposition he continually received from Judaizing teachers who stressed the Mosaic law made this emphasis especially important. The argument is based on the admitted glory of the old covenant, called here "the ministry of death." The text refers to the giving of the law on Sinai with its glorious accompanying circumstances. The old covenant is called the ministry of death because it "kills" (3:6) by placing its offenders under condemnation.

In spite of its death-dealing results, the old covenant was nevertheless a product of God and was initiated with impressive phenomena. One of those remarkable displays was the appearance of Moses' face. When he descended from the mountain, his face shone with a supernatural glow so that he had to put on a veil (see Exod. 34:29-35). Paul reminded his readers, however, that this glorious glow was a fading thing, and later he expanded this thought to symbolize the temporary nature of the old covenant (3:11).

VERSE 8. The question is then asked, to which the answer should be obvious: "Will not the ministry of the Spirit be even more glorious?" (NIV). If the former dispensation had a covenant which ministered death, surely the new covenant which provides regeneration by the Spirit[9] of God (3:3, 6) should be regarded as even more glorious.

VERSE 9. The argument is reinforced by another comparison. Once again Paul argued from the assumption that the old covenant, here termed "the ministry of condemnation," possessed a genuine glory. This was true even though it was a covenant that placed man under condemnation because no one was ever able to keep it perfectly.

The new covenant is a different sort, and not only does not leave its subjects under condemnation, but also provides something positive. Paul called it "the ministry of righteousness" because it supplies its recipients with God's approval instead of condemnation. "Righteousness" is a legal term which denotes the judge's pronouncement that the defendant is acceptable, without any broken law to accuse him. In the new covenant, which is based on Christ's substitutionary death for sinners, all who believe

9. *tou pneumatos* ("of the Spirit") is regarded here as an objective genitive, parallel with the other objective genitives *tou thanatou* ("of death") in 3:7, and *tēs katakriseōs* ("of condemnation") and *tēs dikaiosunēs* ("of righteousness") in 3:9.

are provided with God's verdict of righteousness—His approval and acceptance, based not on the merits of the sinner but on the perfect righteousness of Christ. Surely a ministry that involves such a covenant must abound with glory!

VERSE 10. Paul reached the climax of his argument by pointing to the temporary character of the old covenant and the evident superiority of that new covenant which was planned to take its place. The Greek text at this point does not translate easily into clear English. Both NASB and NIV have paraphrased somewhat, but the idea is made clear. "That which has been glorified" (literal) refers to the old covenant, mediated by Moses, which had certain attendant glories already mentioned. "Has not been glorified in this respect" (literal) indicates some limitation on the glory which the old covenant did have. "The glory that surpasses it" refers to the greater glory of the new covenant which the apostles were ministering. Paul's point was that the glory of the old has been eclipsed by the greater glory of the new. Just as the moon becomes invisible in the overpowering sunlight of the day, so the glory of the old covenant and its ministry has faded away.

VERSE 11. After acknowledging that the law existed with a genuine glory for a time, while at the same time noting that it was a transitory, fading instrument as was the glow on Moses' face (3:7), Paul drew the significant conclusion: How much more should we understand that the new covenant which replaced the former one *remains* in glory. It should be obvious that anything which God has given to supersede a glorious covenant must be even more glorious.

c. The openness of the new covenant (3:12-18)

VERSE 12. The previous references to the fading glory of the old covenant and the experience of Moses led Paul to emphasize another important feature of the new covenant—its openness in contrast to the old.

"Having therefore such a hope" was Paul's statement of assurance that the provisions of the new covenant will all be realized. Therefore, he and his assistants had no hesitancy in proclaiming its truth with great boldness. They were not fearful of the Judaizers, even though it was a startling message to proclaim in Jewish circles that the Mosaic law as a system for God's people had been replaced by another covenant.

VERSE 13. Paul used the incident at Sinai when Moses placed a veil over his face (Exod. 34:33-35) to illustrate his point. The KJV translation of Exodus 34:33 implies that Moses wore the veil while he was speaking with Israel, and then took it off. The supplied word "till" has been corrected to "when" in ASV, NASB, and NIV. The idea of the passage is that Israel was allowed to see the radiant face of Moses when he was conveying God's word to them, but that he covered his face when he was finished. Paul correctly understood the reason to be that Moses did not wish the Israelites to be watching his face each time the glory faded away.[10]

VERSE 14. This dramatic procedure of Moses, however, was confronted by the spiritual hardness of Israelite hearts. Most of them failed to understand the true nature of the glory of Moses' face. Paul explained that the same spiritual dullness existed among the Jews of his day. Just as the veil hid the fading glory of Moses' face from Jewish observers, so the same sort of obscuring veil seemed to hide the true meaning of the old covenant when the Jews read it. They were unable to see that it was transient, that it pointed to Christ, and that it would be replaced by a new covenant.

The obscuring veil of unbelief remains unlifted for Israel because it is removed only in connection with Christ and His work. Only by faith in Him can a person see the glory of the new covenant, as well as the replacement of the old by the new.

VERSE 15. The previous verse described the veil as resting on the old covenant and obscuring the proper understanding of it. Here Paul made it clear that the fault was not with that covenant, but with the people. The veil was actually over their hearts. The old covenant was not misleading. The problem lay in the unbelief of Jewish hearts. This circumstance was true at the writing of II Corinthians, twenty-five years after Christ's resurrection. It still characterizes Israel as a nation more than nineteen centuries later.

VERSE 16. The language of this verse is adapted from Exodus 34:34.

---

10. This is the view of modern commentators. Philip E. Hughes, however, rejects this explanation, and suggests Moses' action as merely intended to prevent Israel from continually beholding even this transient glory because of its sinfulness. *Commentary on the Second Epistle to the Corinthians*, pp. 107-110.

There it described Moses, who took the veil off when he went to speak with the Lord. Paul used that terminology to illustrate what happens when anyone turns to the Lord. Faith in Christ removes the obscuring veil from the heart, and there is open communion with God under the terms of the new covenant as announced in the gospel.

Because no subject is given in the original text for the verb "turns," the KJV has supplied "it," referring presumably to "heart" as the antecedent. NASB supplies "a man" and NIV uses "anyone." Contextually it is likely that "the heart of a Jew" is meant. However, the statement can also be regarded as a general one, "whenever one turns . . . ." The truth is the same for Jew or Gentile: turning to the Lord in faith removes the separating veil of obscurity, and the true understanding of the old covenant can be gained.

VERSE 17. There is a clear relationship of this verse to 3:6 and 8. There it was stated that the new covenant proceeds from the Spirit, it is life-giving, and is more glorious than the old covenant. Paul then illustrated from the life of Moses the transitory character of the old covenant, in contrast to the open, unveiled nature of the new. In this verse he pointed out that the Lord Himself is the Spirit about whom he had been speaking. On the understanding that "the Lord" is a reference to Christ, as was usual with Paul, the thought is that Christ and the Spirit are one in essence, just as Christ and the Father are one (John 10:30) in that mysterious union of the Trinity. In the new covenant Christ brings about the inner transformation of believers by the action of the Spirit (called in 3:3 the Spirit of the living God).

This activity of the Spirit of the Lord brings liberty, not deadness (3:6) or bondage. New birth by the Spirit has infused believers with new life, and brings freedom from enslavement to sin's guilt and power (Gal. 5:1-5).

VERSE 18. Consequently all Christians, not just the apostles, behold God's glory with an unveiled face. Because they have turned to the Lord, the veil has been removed from their understanding and they have open access to the revelation of God in Christ.

Our versions vary between the concepts of "beholding as in a mirror" (NASB) or "reflecting" ("And we, who . . . reflect," NIV) as translations for a Greek word appearing only this once in the New Testament.[11] Although the

11. The verb *katoptrizō* in the active means "to produce a reflection" and in the middle

idea of reflecting fits the parallel with Moses who reflected the glory of God, the translation "beholding" is usually preferred. The ancient versions commonly understood it this way. There is no clear instance of the verb having the meaning "reflect" unless it is in the active voice (it is middle here). Furthermore, the passage speaks of believers who can now see clearly because the veil has been removed from them.

With faces (and hearts) unveiled, believers may behold the glory of God as they are brought into relationship with Him through Christ (see also 4:6). Those who press the imagery may identify the mirror as the Word, or Christ. Inasmuch as mirrors in Paul's day were polished metal that gave somewhat imperfect images, the thought is explained as indicating that even though our vision of Christ's glory is vastly superior to the Old Testament experiences, it is still something less than the final vision when we see Him face to face (I Cor. 13:12; I John 3:2). It is not necessary, however, to push the interpretation this far, since the emphasis in the statement is not on the mirror but on the beholding.

As believers behold the Lord's glory, now that the veil of spiritual dullness is removed, they are continually being transformed[12] into His image. The word describes a change of form which is intrinsic. The true nature of the child of God is progressively revealed, just as the process of metamorphosis transforms a caterpillar into a butterfly. Paul referred to the progressive sanctification of believers whereby, as they behold Christ and increase in their understanding of Him, they become more and more like Him, from one stage of glory to the next. We perceive Christ's glory as we seek spiritual nourishment in the Word of God, the Scripture. The transformation is then accomplished in us supernaturally by the Lord, identified here as the Spirit. The Holy Spirit gives the new covenant its distinctive character (3:6, 8). No wonder the apostle exulted as he did at being involved in Christian ministry which could accomplish such a feat.

"to look at oneself in a mirror." It is the middle voice which appears in 3:18. Arndt, pp. 425–26; G. Kittel, TDNT, II, 696.

12. The present tense of the verb *metamorphoumetha* denotes progressive action.

Questions for Discussion

1. In what way is Christian ministry sometimes an aroma of death?
2. What instances can you describe of persons "peddling the word of God"?
3. Why did Moses put a veil over his face?
4. What features about the Mosaic covenant did Paul illustrate from the incident of the veil?
5. How does God accomplish the progressive transformation of believers?

4

Some Obstacles to the Ministry

II Corinthians 4

The glory of Christian ministry which Paul had been describing did not, however, mean that ministry always enjoyed uninterrupted successes. Its glory pertained chiefly to its spiritual significance, and not everyone sees this feature. Those who tend to judge the value of anything solely by immediate results, trappings of success, or by physical and temporal benefits need to realize another aspect of true Christian ministry.

The sobering fact is that Christian ministry is faced with obstacles. The accomplishment of God's work is no easy task. Paul informed the church that his own ministry was beset with various accusations and criticisms. Furthermore, he and his assistants lived constantly under the threat of death. Their physical bodies were paying the price for their commitment to this ministry. The secret of their steadfastness lay in their unshakable faith in God's revealed truth and in the eternal value of Christ's cause. In this vein Paul continued the description of the character of his ministry which he began in 2:14.

4. The ministry was carried out openly (4:1-6)

VERSE 1. This paragraph not only is a positive assertion of the openness and candor with which Paul and his assistants had ministered, but also seems to be a response to criticism leveled against him by certain Corinthians (see 1:12, 17; 3:1).

"This ministry" to which Paul referred was the ministry of the new covenant (3:6). It was the task of proclaiming and teaching the gospel of Christ, the glorious news that sins have been forgiven through Christ's death, and that His perfect righteousness has been made available to those who will trust Him for it. Paul had previously disclaimed any personal adequacy that had made him worthy of this responsibility (3:5). Once again he evidenced deep humility by saying "we received mercy" in being given such a task. Does this imply that some of the religious peddlers at Corinth (2:17) were suggesting that Paul and his associates were too highhanded or authoritarian when they preached among them? Then let them know that Paul's ministry was no display of ego or personal vanity, but the response of one who viewed his position as an instance of God's mercy on undeserving men.

Consequently, Paul and his men did not "lose heart" (*enkakoumen*). In spite of accusations and difficulties, they continued performing their ministry without cowardice or discouragement. A firm conviction of the nature of their mission kept them going.

VERSE 2. Paul claimed an openness about his ministry with complete absence of any sort of secrecy or subterfuge. There had been a renunciation or disowning of those things which one hides because of a sense of shame.[1] As ministers of God, there had been no trickery in their methods or their message. They had done no falsifying or adulterating of the Word of God when they proclaimed the gospel. They were not guilty of giving wrong emphases or withholding significant parts of truth.

Again, one can imagine that certain criticisms of Paul may be alluded to here. Had Judaizing teachers accused him of omitting certain teachings regarding compliance with Mosaic rites? Were they accusing him of enticing Gentiles with a watered-down message of salvation at the outset, with the scheme in mind of adding the other essentials later? Paul's clear answer was that the Word of God had been handled in such a way as to

1. This is Arndt's translation of *ta krupta tēs aischunēs* ("the hidden things of shame"). The translation "hidden things of dishonesty" (KJV) reflects the obsolete English usage of "dishonest" in the sense of "shameful."

display its truth to every open-minded listener. It had been taught not only for intellectual stimulation, but its moral and spiritual implications also had been clearly aimed at the conscience of each hearer. This in turn should have commended the preachers themselves to the conscience of every Corinthian as being faithful messengers of God. These words reflect no self-seeking on Paul's part, but rather were his solemn recognition that his ministry was carried on "in the sight of God," who not only was guiding his labors but also was enlightening the consciences of those who were open to His truth. How refreshing it would be if it could be said of every preacher that his chief commendation is his fidelity to the truth of God's Word and the impact which he makes on the consciences of his hearers.

VERSE 3. Paul recognized, however, that not everyone responds favorably to the gospel. The reference to "every man's conscience" (4:2) was a generalization with many exceptions. "Even if our gospel is veiled" (NASB, NIV) states a condition which he was willing for the moment to assume as true.[2] He quickly explained, however, that the problem was not with the gospel nor its preachers but with the unbelieving hearers. It is veiled to "those who are perishing." Paul moved in his metaphor from the veil over the face of Moses (3:13) to the veil over the heart of Israel (3:15), and now the veil over the gospel as far as unbelievers are concerned.

VERSE 4. This veiling of the gospel was not because Paul had used secrecy in his preaching or deviousness in his methods. Rather it was because the thoughts of perishing unbelievers had been blinded by the "god of this world." The reference is to Satan, who elsewhere is called by the similar titles "prince of this world" (John 12:31; 14:30; 16:11) and "prince of the power of the air" (Eph. 2:2). He is "god," not in any dualistic sense as equal to and independent of the true God, but only in the limited sense that his followers so regard him, and at present God allows him to utilize this power over the minds of sinners.

Because of Satan's action in blinding the minds of sinners, they are not able to see the illumination of the glory of Christ which the gospel provides. The good news about Jesus Christ as Lord, His unique person,

2. A first class condition, using *ei* with the indicative mood.

His stupendous works, and His incomparable teachings—all are minimized, explained away, or otherwise perverted so that sinners disregard the
spiritual enlightenment which could save their souls from destruction. The
glory of Christ is essentially His unique person as the image of God, the
One who is the revealer of the invisible God (John 1:18; Col. 1:15), on whom
men must depend if they would see the Father (John 14:9) and receive
salvation.

VERSE 5. Paul would not let his readers escape the real issue involved in
Christian ministry. His ministry was not a promotion of the preacher,
directly or indirectly. He and his associates had never preached themselves.
The heart of their ministering the gospel was their proclamation of Jesus
Christ as Lord.[3] This acknowledgment is basic to the gospel (Rom. 10:9;
I Cor. 12:3), and thus lay at the heart of Paul's message. One should beware
of drawing categorical distinctions between accepting Christ as Savior and
accepting Him as Lord. Both are clearly involved in any true commitment
to Christ.

Just as Paul had been faithful in presenting Christ as Lord in his
preaching, so he and his associates had been careful to maintain their own
position as servants among the Corinthians. He did not mean that the
Corinthians were the masters, for Christ was the Master whom they served.
But Paul did mean that as Christ's servants, he and his associates had
followed His orders and that had involved ministering to the Corinthians.

VERSE 6. The messengers gave no thought to promoting themselves
because of the overwhelming grandeur of the source from which their
message came. God, who had once brought physical light out of darkness
by His creative command (Gen. 1:3), had Himself shone with spiritual
enlightenment in the hearts of believers. At creation light resulted from a
command of God. At regeneration God Himself shines as the illumination.

This light from God is explained as the knowledge of God as revealed in
the face of Jesus Christ. Sin hardens the heart (3:14), makes it unbelieving

3. Word order suggests that *kurion* should be regarded as a predicate usage, "Jesus Christ
as Lord." If it were simply part of the title, one would have expected it to be first in the series:
"Lord Jesus Christ."

Fig. 5. Lechaion Street, leading to the agora of ancient Corinth.

and insensitive to God (3:16), and is utilized by Satan to keep men in the spiritual darkness of unbelief (4:4). The great mission of Christ is His role as the image of God to reveal the Father's glory to men when they have a spiritual encounter with His Son.

For Paul this transforming encounter had occurred on the Damascus road more than twenty years earlier. At that time he had been struck down with an overpowering light and had seen the glorious Lord who identified Himself as Jesus (Acts 9:1-9; 22:5-11; 26:12-18). Some of the phenomena of that occasion probably influenced Paul's language here ("light," "glory of God," "face of Christ"). However, one must not limit the thrust of this verse to the miraculous physical happenings on that day. The use of the plural "our hearts" shows that more than one person was in the apostle's thought, and the reference to God's action of shining in "hearts" applies to the spiritual experience of every believer.

5. The ministry was performed, however, in bodily
   weakness (4:7—5:10)

   a. Present trials of God's messenger (4:7-12)

VERSE 7. Paul's ministry of proclaiming the new covenant (3:6) carried with it certain burdens. Not the least of them was the presence of various trials which God's messengers must undergo. "This treasure" refers to the light of the knowledge of God in Christ as explained in the preceding verse. This sublime truth is contained, however, in "earthen vessels" ("jars of clay," NIV). The metaphor depicts pottery jars used as storage for all sorts of items. Household lamps were made of clay to hold oil and a wick. Valuables were stored in such jars. The Dead Sea Scrolls were found in pottery jars after being hidden for nineteen centuries. Paul used the figure to depict either the human body with its frailties, or perhaps the entire human personality[4] inasmuch as body, soul, and spirit are a unity, and all are subject to weakness, suffering, and discouragement.

Paul wanted no mistake to be made about the true nature of the Christian message in comparison to the significance of the minister. The human instrument is weak and expendable; the message is vital and of inestimable value. By utilizing frail human ministers, God demonstrates that the "surpassing greatness of the power" which transforms men's lives is from God and not from any preacher.

VERSE 8. In a series of four contrasting parallels, Paul showed what he and other true ministers were continually facing. "Troubled on every side, yet not distressed" (KJV) also has been translated "hard pressed . . . but not crushed" (NIV). The idea is that in spite of pressures that would thwart their effectiveness, these ministers were never completely crushed so that their ministry totally failed. In Paul's ministry such experiences were multiplied. At Philippi, for example, he was arrested and imprisoned; yet the gospel was not stopped, for the jailer and his household were converted

---

4. Alfred Plummer, *Corinthians Two*, p. 127.

(Acts 16). At Corinth he had been arrested and accused before the provincial governor, but dismissal of the case gave new opportunities for the gospel.

"Perplexed, but not despairing" is a play on words[5] which is not easily preserved in English. One commentator has rendered it "being at a loss, but not having lost out."[6] These contrasting phrases emphasize human inability as offset by divine enablement. Perhaps Paul was thinking of experiences like his recent one at Ephesus, where the riot in the city left him powerless to act, and yet God preserved his Christian witness (Acts 19).

VERSE 9. Paul and his associates were continually being persecuted by opponents of the Christian message, but the Lord who sent them never abandoned them. At different times one group or another persecuted Paul; he was frequently a hunted man (Acts 9:23-24, 28-29; 13:50; 14:5-6, 19-20; et al.). Yet never did Paul and his coworkers conclude that God had forsaken them, and for this reason they continued their ministry. From time to time adversaries might succeed in casting them down, but never would this result in their destruction before their mission was accomplished. God's enablement was still in operation, even though His messengers faced great obstacles.

VERSE 10. Here Paul began an explanation of the preceding paradoxes. The sufferings which the apostolic party experienced, along with the successful accomplishment of its mission in spite of impending disaster, must be interpreted as Paul indicated. Their sufferings were actually a "carrying about in the body the dying of Jesus." The next verse (4:11) is parallel in thought and makes it clear that Paul was considering Christ's physical sufferings and death. Paul and the other apostles were constantly under threat of physical death just as Jesus was. Now the hatred of men for the Son of God was being directed against Paul and others as they attempted to carry out their Christian ministry. The word "dying" (*nekrōsin*) does not mean simply death but the process of dying. Paul chose this term

5. Greek: *aporoumenoi all' ouk exaporoumenoi.*
6. R. C. H. Lenski, *Interpretation of First and Second Corinthians,* pp. 977-978.

to emphasize not just one act, but the repeated sufferings which were directed against his life in order to put him to death.

Nevertheless Paul could look beyond the trials to the grander purpose which was being served. God's suffering servants not only showed their identification with Christ by their willingness to suffer as He did, but they also displayed His life in their bodies. Christ living in them enabled them not to be crushed, be despairing, feel forsaken, or be destroyed. They ran the risk of death in order to proclaim the new life in Christ, and they did this by personal demonstration of Christ's life in their own lives.

VERSE 11. In this parallel expression, Paul's meaning in the preceding verse is more fully explained. As ministers of Christ he and the other apostles were continually exposed to the danger of physical death. This was what Paul meant by carrying about in his body "the dying of Jesus." He had learned at the very beginning of his Christian life that persecution directed against Christians was regarded by Jesus as actually against Him (Acts 9:4-5; cf. Col. 1:24). The purpose, however, was not to undergo suffering for suffering's sake, but that "the life of Jesus also may be manifested in our mortal flesh." The proclamation of the new life in Christ became more clearly manifested when it was set forth against such a dramatic background. The eternal life provided by Jesus, who said "I am . . . the life" (John 14:6), enabled His messengers to be victorious in spite of physical weakness, and would ultimately make them triumphant even though many of them would experience a martyr's death.

VERSE 12. In summation, death was an ever-present reality with Christ's messengers, but His purposes were being accomplished because eternal life was being received by the Corinthians and others who had responded to the gospel.

Paul was not describing explicitly the experience of every Christian in this passage, but primarily that of himself and the other apostles. In the context he was not talking about the Corinthians, but about those who had preached to them. Nevertheless the principle was set forth that God's servants have His truth in earthen vessels that are fragile and subject to damage. By application of this principle every Christian may recognize that physical weakness and opposition from adversaries can cause hardship in the performance of any Christian ministry.

b. Importance of faith to God's messenger (4:13-18)

VERSE 13. It must not be supposed, however, that Paul's previous words were a bitter complaint about the personal difficulties of his ministry. What sustained him and his companions was the same viewpoint and attitude which the psalmist expressed in Psalm 116:10, "I believed; therefore I said" (NIV). The context of these words in the psalm reveals the writer to have been in great adversity (116:3, 6, 8). Yet his faith in God caused him to pray for deliverance (116:4), and he continued to bear his testimony, believing that God ultimately brings vindication to His saints whether in this life or the next (116:2, 9, 10, 15). This same "spirit of faith"[7] permeated Paul and his suffering companions. Because they had an abiding faith in God who had revealed His Son to them, they continued to preach the gospel in spite of continual risk and frequent affliction.

VERSE 14. A firm faith in the resurrection made Paul willing to risk death in order to carry out his ministry. He was convinced that the Father had raised Jesus, for Paul had seen Him on the Damascus road. He also firmly believed that Christ's resurrection had guaranteed the resurrection of all others who were united to Him by faith. Consequently no fear of death could divert him from his mission of proclaiming the new covenant that God has provided for men (3:6).

Does it seem that Paul had expected to avoid death through the rapture (I Thess. 4:13-18) but had become resigned to dying and looked only to the resurrection? It is better to understand Paul's view as exactly what our Lord had taught: namely, that His coming is imminent but unpredictable. Every believer should be ready at all times for death or the rapture. We should long for the Lord's return and the prospect of meeting Him by whatever route He may require of us.

7. Some interpreters explain this phrase as "the Spirit of faith," a direct reference to the Holy Spirit; others have suggested an indirect reference to the Spirit as the bestower of a gift of faith. However, the expression is more generally understood here as denoting a spiritual state or disposition. Compare the similar phrase of Paul, "a spirit of meekness" (I Cor. 4:21; Gal. 6:1, KJV).

VERSE 15. So firm was Paul's faith that he could look with joy at the outcome of his labors, even though they were being done at tremendous cost. "All things" that he and other ministers were undergoing were for the benefit of the Corinthians and other Christians. His eye of faith saw beyond the immediate trials. He saw God's saving grace being multiplied through a continuous stream of new converts. As the grace of God in the gospel was received by more and more people, the thanksgiving of their grateful hearts would overflow and bring glory to God. It was faith that enabled him to have God's perspective.

VERSE 16. In spite of great obstacles, therefore, Paul and his associates did not "lose heart" (*enkakoumen*). The same verb is used in 4:1. No amount of discouragement could make Paul abandon his mission. He freely admitted that his "outer man" was decaying. He had previously spoken of physical life as "earthen vessels" (4:7) and would later refer to it as an "earthly tent" (5:1). Furthermore, the hardships of travel and the heavy burden of the care of the churches placed great strain on his physical body. His various imprisonments, beatings, and continual harassments had left their scars.

Of far greater significance in Paul's eyes was the "inner man," and here the story was far different. His inner man was being renewed as each day passed. The reference is to the Christian's regenerated spiritual existence which can grow stronger in spite of physical weakness. This inner man is also called by Paul the "new man" (Col. 3:10, KJV) and is described as experiencing continuous renewal as believers increase in their understanding of God through the enlightenment of the Holy Spirit (Eph. 3:16). As Paul's Christian life progressed toward its inevitable earthly close, his physical capacities might lessen but his spiritual awareness of God's program continued to develop. He understood more clearly the values which should govern the Christian's outlook, and he shared them with his readers.

VERSE 17. Because of the spiritual insight which his inner man now understood, Paul could refer to his incredible trials as "momentary, light affliction." Humanly considered they could have been regarded far differently, and Paul himself did not minimize their severity (4:8-12). Yet Paul here was looking at them in the light of Romans 8:28 and the eternal purposes of God. He understood that, severe as his sufferings were, they were momentary and light in comparison to the "eternal weight of glory" which lies ahead for all who trust the Lord and serve Him faithfully. "Weight" (*baros*) is probably used in contrast to "light" or "lightness" (*elaphron*). Human assessment would call physical affliction a heavy weight. Paul said his difficulties were actually light in comparison to the glory that "far outweighs them all" (NIV). Faith enabled him to view his life this way.

VERSE 18. This statement gives the essence of Paul's ability to see the glory of Christian ministry rather than to be disillusioned by the obstacles. He and others like him had learned not to focus their gaze on things which are seen, but to fix their attention with eyes of faith on things which are not seen. They had learned the basic truth that the matters of this present world, including even the most serious of human afflictions, are only transitory. The unseen things of the spiritual life are of eternal value. The regenerated life, the continuing ministry of the Spirit, the growing comprehension of God through daily communion with Him, the promises of God for the present and the future—all of these and many more are things not seen, but they are just as real as the visible objects of this world and are far more permanent. With this kind of spiritual emphasis in Paul's life, no earthly obstacle could blur his vision of the glory of serving Christ.

Questions for Discussion

1. In what sense is Satan the god of this world? Are there any limitations? Give scriptural evidence for your answers.
2. Why does God sometimes allow His ministers to suffer unusual hardships?
3. How did Paul display both the dying and the life of Jesus in his body?
4. Did Paul expect to be alive when Christ returns? Give the reasons for your answer.
5. What are some practical ways in which faith helped you through a difficult time?

5

The Motivation of the Ministry

II Corinthians 5

The apostle Paul had been writing about the ministry which Christ gave him. He had described the message which he was commissioned to proclaim—a message that brings new life to believers. He had spoken of the glory he saw in this ministry, and also of the hardships and obstacles which he had faced as he tried to be faithful to his calling. He made it clear that he could press forward only if he concentrated on spiritual goals. His eye of faith was focused on eternal issues, not on this world's passing scene (4:18).

What was it that kept Paul dedicated and faithful in spite of minimal earthly rewards, great danger, and possible death? His motivation must have been incredibly strong. Learning what kept Paul committed to his ministry can help other Christians to evaluate their own motives and priorities in their service for Christ. These matters occupied Paul's attention in this portion of his letter.

c. The Christian hope after death (5:1-10)

(1) The prospect at death (5:1-5)

VERSE 1. The thought is clearly related to the preceding discussion in 4:7-18. Paul's ministry was aggravated by many trials, including bodily weaknesses. He extended himself in his efforts to minister helpfully to the Corinthians and others to such a degree that death was working in him

(4:12), and his body exhibited some signs of approaching death (4:10). Nevertheless he had the proper attitude toward the prospect of death, and this was due to his understanding of what lies in store for believers when death comes.

The "earthly house of this tabernacle" (KJV) has been translated more clearly as "the earthly tent which is our house" (NASB) or "the earthly tent we live in" (NIV). The phrase refers to our physical bodies, and emphasizes their temporary nature. Paul's trade as a tentmaker (Acts 18:3) readily suggested the metaphor. A tent was easily dismantled (*kataluthēi*), in contrast to a more permanent structure like a house. Here Paul referred to the destruction of physical bodies by physical death.

In contrast to this temporary "tent," believers have a "building from God." It is a house "not made with hands." Inasmuch as it might be said that physical bodies are not made with hands either, another explanation is needed. The answer is found in Hebrews 9:11, where the expression is explained as meaning "not a part of this creation" (NIV). Hence Paul referred to a building that is not part of this present physical creation. It is rather in the heavens and is eternal.

What is this building from God? Much discussion has been devoted to this passage. Three possible identifications deserve mention. Some commentators see here a reference to heaven itself, or to the believer's "mansion" in heaven (John 14:2, KJV). However, this does not offer as clear a parallel to the physical body. One expects something more closely personal, that with which the believer is clothed (5:2) and without which he is naked (5:3). A second view, by far the commonest, sees the building as a reference to the resurrection body. This is properly analogous to the physical body which is destroyed at death, and answers the contextual terminology regarding being clothed and not being naked. This opinion sees Paul as viewing death transcended by resurrection, in agreement with his discussion in I Corinthians 15. It does not, however, take any notice of the intermediate state of the believer between death and resurrection.

A third view sees here a possible reference to an intermediate body which the believer has until the resurrection. One should not be dogmatic about this because the biblical evidence is not certain; however, this passage could be interpreted in this manner. To see here a reference to an intermediate body would answer Paul's concern that the loss of his physical body by death would leave him naked. If the "building from God" is the resurrection body, then he *would be* naked until the resurrection. Furthermore, there is some biblical evidence for intermediate bodies between death and resurrection. Moses and Elijah were not disembodied spirits at the transfiguration, but did possess visible bodies (Matt. 17:3, et al.). The martyrs of the tribulation wore white robes after their deaths but prior to their resurrection (Rev. 6:9-11). If anyone questions that an intermediate body would by definition not be "eternal" as this verse states, the answer could be found in the similar terminology used regarding the kingdom. It is described as lasting one thousand years (Rev. 20:1-5), and at other times as being eternal (Rev. 11:15). Apparently it merges into the eternal state and yet its basic character is not significantly changed.

VERSE 2. It is indeed true that we groan as long as we are in the physical body[1] with its susceptibility to ailments, injury, and death. Paul had already described some of his personal experiences in this regard (4:7-18). Nevertheless there was light at the end of the tunnel, and this kept him pressing on. Death would be no catastrophe, for his new dwelling from heaven would be vastly superior. Whether this prospective dwelling is interpreted as the resurrection body or as an intermediate body, the point is the same: eternal things are worthy of our concentration, and should motivate us to serve Christ in hope.

VERSE 3. The reason[2] Paul longed for his new body was not only that it will replace a temporary and mortal one, but also that it will solve the problem of being "found naked" (NASB, NIV), which he clearly abhorred. If he referred to the resurrection body, the state of nakedness for the soul between death and resurrection would be finally ended; if he were thinking of those still alive at Christ's return, no disembodied state would need to

1. "In this" (*en toutōi*) has no expressed object for the preposition, but the most obvious word to be supplied is the "earthly tent" of 5:1, referring to the mortal body.

2. The meaning "inasmuch as" for *ei ge* is supported by Arndt, p. 152.

occur. If this verse refers to an intermediate body, a naked state would be prevented.

VERSE 4. "We [who] are in this tent" refers to persons still alive in their physical bodies. They "groan" and are "burdened," not in the Platonic sense that the body itself is evil and should be abandoned, but because of the sufferings to which it is subject. The reason, Paul said, is not that we wish to be unclothed. He had no morbid thoughts. Death for its own sake is not to be desired. It is still an enemy (I Cor. 15:26). Paul did not imply that the body must be put off at all costs. What he longed for was its replacement by a superior body. Ultimately that will be the resurrection body, and the terminology of the mortal being swallowed up by life is similar to that used in I Corinthians 15:54.

VERSE 5. The encouraging factor which prompted these strong convictions about the future is God Himself who has prepared believers for this glorious prospect. It is He who has called us and made us new creatures, and has arranged our resurrection.

Furthermore, He has given every believer the Holy Spirit as the pledge or deposit that assures us of final fulfillment. The term "earnest" (*arrabōn*) was a legal and commercial term denoting a first installment, deposit, down payment, or pledge. It paid a part of the purchase price in advance, this securing a legal claim to the item at issue and making the contract valid.[3] By supplying believers with the Spirit, God has given a foretaste of the life to come, has created a longing for full realization, and has guaranteed that the rest will follow.

(2) The confidence of the apostle (5:6-8)

VERSE 6. "Therefore" (*oun*) indicates a logical connection with the preceding material. It was in view of Paul's possession of the Spirit who provided complete assurance of the future life and resurrection that he could say of himself and his associates "being always of good courage" (*tharrountes oun pantote*). It was not blind foolhardiness but knowledgeable confidence.

3. Arndt, p. 109.

Furthermore, Paul put the proper evaluation on these factors. He understood that being "at home in the body," that is, being alive physically, meant being (in a literal translation) "away from home from the Lord."[4] This puts physical life, death, and the life to come in their true perspective. The proper and ultimate home for the believer is with Christ, and this fact should govern Christian attitudes on these issues. Of course, Paul was not denying the fact of the Lord's presence with believers in this life, but he was speaking of the more direct personal presence when we see Him face to face (cf. I John 3:2).

VERSE 7. This is a parenthetical statement, enlarging on the nature of the present life which is absent from the Lord. The point of the parenthesis is that during this "absent" period, the blessed realities of the life to come must be accepted by faith. We cannot yet look on their actual form or appearance (*eidous*). Nevertheless, the ministry of Christ has been thoroughly witnessed and reported by reliable observers, and the Holy Spirit has brought inner conviction and assurance. The walk by faith, therefore, is a reasonable procedure for the person who knows God.

VERSE 8. The thought of verse 6 is now resumed and taken forward. Not only did Paul retain his courage in view of the prospects that lie beyond death for the Christian, but he also preferred to be at home with the Lord. It should be noted that he did not state that he preferred to be dead, but that his preference was "to be away from home from the body and at home with the Lord" (literal). This was no morbid death wish, but a triumphant expression of faith that looked beyond present sufferings to the ultimate glory.

(3) The incentive of coming judgment (5:9-10)

VERSE 9. As Paul thought of the prospect of death, he reflected also on the implications of judgment and the incentive which this provides for Christian living. "We have as our ambition,"[5] he said, to be pleasing to the

4. A play is made on the words *endēmountes* ("being at home") and *ekdēmoumen* ("away from home").

5. The verb *philotimeomai* occurs only in Romans 15:20, II Corinthians 5:9, and I Thessalonians 4:11 in the New Testament. Such translations as "have as one's ambition," "consider it an honor," or "aspire," are better than "labour" (KJV). Arndt, p. 869.

Lord. He wanted to be pleasing, "whether at home or away from home" (literal). In the light of the context where these words have just been used (5:6, 8), it is almost certain that the reference is to being "at home in the body" (NIV; that is, physically alive) or "away from home from the body" (literal; that is, physically dead). Inasmuch as the idea of seeking to please Christ during the intermediate state ("away from home") introduces a contradiction with the statement in 5:10 where this pleasing of Christ had to do with deeds done in the body, one must understand the thought in some other way. It is best to understand that Paul's ambition to please Christ was unaffected by the prospect of being either alive or dead when Christ returns. Either way, whether he should be living and caught up to meet the Lord in the air, or would be resurrected from the dead, his aim was to live in a way that pleased his Lord.

VERSE 10. Paul reminded his readers that all believers must appear before the judgment seat of Christ. He was not speaking of a general judgment of all mankind, but a judgment of Christians. Furthermore, he was not describing a penal judgment that will determine a person's final destiny, but an examination of believers' works which will determine rewards.

The Corinthians were familiar with the Roman judgment seat (*bēma*), for their city had one in the agora (marketplace). The *bēma* was a raised stone platform where the governor conducted legal business, and where victorious athletes were rewarded (see Fig. 6). Paul had earlier appeared before Gallio at the Corinthian *bēma* and had his case dismissed (Acts 18:12-17).

At the judgment seat of Christ, He will examine the service which the believer has performed while in his physical body. Another description of this judgment by Paul occurs in I Corinthians 3:10-15. One must be careful not to confuse this judgment with the punishment of sin, for justification has cared for all of that (Acts 13:39) and believers are no longer under condemnation (Rom. 8:1). Salvation itself is not an issue here. At the same time, the seriousness of the judgment seat of Christ should not be minimized. "Saved . . . so as by fire" (I Cor. 3:15, KJV) does not depict a totally pleasant experience.

Fig. 6. Bema (judgment seat) at Corinth.

It is clear that each believer is accountable to Christ for the worth of his actions in the body, "whether good or bad." The believer's deeds which Christ will pronounce "good" will bring a reward (I Cor. 3:14). What sort of recompense will be given for those deeds which will be seen as "bad"? Inasmuch as Christ's death rendered payment for all the sins of all believers, this statement cannot mean that punishment will be meted out for the believer's sins. To exempt unconfessed sins of the believer from the expiatory work of Christ is to deny many clear passages of Scripture (Ps. 103:12; Heb. 8:12; 10:12, 14).

It is far better to understand the recompense for what is "bad" to mean that unfaithfulness will go unrewarded. Furthermore, there will be a sense of shame before Christ as such believers see their worthless works destroyed (I Cor. 3:15), and respond with true remorse (I John 2:28).

Nevertheless, the prevailing mood at this judgment will be one of joy and gratitude. No tears will permanently mar the eternal bliss (Rev. 21:4). This fits well with the metaphor of the Grecian *bēma,* where victorious athletes were crowned. As Samuel L. Hoyt has observed: "The judge at the *bēma* bestowed rewards to the victors. *He did not whip the losers.*"[6]

6. The ministry persuaded men from a proper
   motivation (5:11-21)

   a. The motivation of Paul's ministry (5:11-15)

   VERSE 11. As Paul continued his description of his ministry, he concentrated on the matter of motivation and explained what his motivation really was, in contrast to what some people were saying about him. "The fear (*phobon*) of the Lord"[7] is not the terror of the unbeliever which causes sinners to shrink from the impending doom. It is rather the godly respect for the awesome character of God which made Paul take with proper seriousness the responsibilities of the ministry in the light of the judgment seat of Christ (5:10).

   The next two clauses are contrasting parallels and should be taken together: "We persuade men, but we are made manifest to God." It is not directly stated what it is that Paul persuaded men about; therefore, it must be deduced from the context. In the light of the next verse, it is most likely that Paul referred to his integrity as a minister, a matter which was apparently disputed by some detractors at Corinth, but which was clear to God. Paul could only hope that his pure motives would be as clearly recognized by the consciences of his Corinthian readers.

   VERSE 12. This extended discussion was not given for the purpose of promoting Paul. He had denied such a purpose in 3:1, and again he disavowed any such aim. The problem had been caused by the Corinthians themselves. What he was doing, therefore, was giving them "an occasion to be proud of us." He was providing answers for his loyal Corinthian friends to use against his detractors. The opposers were ones who "take pride in

   6. Samuel L. Hoyt, "The Judgment Seat of Christ and Unconfessed Sins," p. 37.
   7. The KJV misleads by the translation "terror."

appearance, and not in heart." They gloried in external, superficial appearances, rather than the deeper motivations and attitudes of the heart. Hence they must have discounted the value of Paul's ministry in favor of themselves or of other teachers. This feature will be dealt with at greater length in chapters 10-13 but the thought is introduced at this point.[8]

VERSE 13. This verse probably continued Paul's rejoinder to the comments of his critics. When they said he was beside himself,[9] perhaps because of his strong preaching, the true explanation was to be found in his zeal for God. A similar charge had been leveled against Jesus (Mark 3:21). At a later time Festus, the Roman governor of Judea, would also say this of Paul (Acts 26:24). When the opposite comment was made—that he was of sound mind—his serious demeanor was for the benefit of the Corinthians. If this latter comment was a criticism that he was too serious about some matters, his answer implied that it was for the Corinthians' safeguarding, and not from any unreliable vacillation.

VERSE 14. The apostle moved to his other emphasis, the love of Christ, which motivated his ministry. Is this referring to Paul's love for Christ, or his recognition of Christ's love for him? A study of Paul's grammatical usage indicates that he always used the subjective genitive when he used the word *agapē* ("love") and then referred to a person.[10] Hence the meaning here must be Christ's love for men. This recognition of Christ's love so controlled Paul that it was hemming him in on all sides.[11] This love provided such strong motivation because he had drawn the proper conclusion from the evidence ("having concluded this"). Christ had died for all men, and therefore all men had died. Paul referred to the death of Christ at Calvary, a death sufficient to pay the penalty for all the sins of all men.

VERSE 15. In this abbreviated statement Paul assumed that identification with Christ in His death involved also an identification with Christ in

8. This refutes the notion of the disunity of the epistle based on the alleged difference in tone between chapters 10-13 and the rest of the letter.

9. Murray J. Harris lists five possible explanations of this statement. "2 Corinthians," *Expositor's Bible Commentary,* X, 351.

10. J. H. Bernard, "The Second Epistle to the Corinthians," EGT, III, 69.

11. Greek: *sunechei,* from *sunecho,* "to hold together, compress."

His resurrection (see the similar discussion in Romans 6:4-11). "They who live" allows for the fact that not all men appropriate by faith the benefits of Christ's death for them, and thus not all become recipients of new life in Christ. Because Christians are dependent on Christ, they should spend their new lives in ways that honor Him. It was this fact that compelled Paul and his associates to devote their lives to Christian ministry.

b. The message of Paul's ministry (5:16-21)

VERSE 16. The basis for Paul's motivation to carry out his ministry lay in the sublime truth that had gripped his heart. That truth was the revelation of what God had done for man through Christ. His ministry was centered on the proclamation of that message.

In the time since Paul had become a believer, he had learned not to assess anyone "according to the flesh" (*kata sarka*). His outlook had been changed and he no longer looked at others from a purely human standpoint. It is common for people to judge one another by such human and external standards as wealth, race, family, personality, and skills. Paul conceded that there was a time when he and others had regarded Christ through a purely human evaluation.[12] They thought of Him as a religious teacher from Galilee, untrained in any rabbinical school, who made messianic claims and was alleged to work miracles. Now, however, Paul no longer regarded Christ from this "worldly point of view" (NIV). By becoming Christians, believers have come to know Christ with the enlightenment of the Spirit.

VERSE 17. The Christian is in vital union with Christ, and this makes him not merely a reformed person but a new creation. Eternal life has been imparted to him, not just a promised extension of earthly life. "The old things passed away." The unregenerate life with the old nature in control is no longer the description of any true believer. Instead, "new things have come." The believer is different, for new elements have been added. The

12. This has nothing to do with whether Paul ever saw Jesus during His earthly ministry. The phrase *kata sarka* ("according to the flesh") should be connected in thought adverbially with *egnōkamen* ("we have known") rather than adjectivally with *Christon* ("Christ").

new Master rules one's life, and one's outlook is different. Spiritual matters become crucial, where once the sinner was dead to them.

VERSE 18. All of this dramatic change is derived from God. It is He "who reconciled us to Himself through Christ" (NASB, NIV). "Reconciled" (*katallaxantos*) means "changed completely," and refers to God's act of changing man's relation to Him by removing, through Christ's work at Calvary, the barrier caused by sin. This is the objective side of reconciliation. It makes salvation possible. However, reconciliation in the New Testament is not precisely the same thing as salvation. This aspect of reconciliation makes salvation possible for man by paying sin's penalty and thus removing this obstacle, but it does not save everybody. Christ's death was sufficient for all, but not all are saved, for the benefits of Christ's death are applied only to those who believe. Thus there is also a subjective side of reconciliation. For this reason God who reconciled all things (that is, changed completely their position in relation to Him) has given the message of reconciliation to His servants. They are to proclaim the gospel, announcing God's reconciliation of man and urging people to accept the gospel and thus be reconciled to Him (see 5:20; also Col. 1:20-22).

VERSE 19. This verse elaborates the content of the "ministry of reconciliation" just mentioned. Interpreters differ as to whether the verb (*ēn . . . katallasōn,* "was . . . reconciling") should be regarded as a periphrastic imperfect with the prepositional phrase attached, "was reconciling in Christ"; or whether the two parts should be separated (as in the Greek text), with *ēn* ("was") used absolutely, "God was in Christ, reconciling . . . ." Greek grammar allows either. If the former is adopted, the point is that God's act of reconciling the world was done in Christ. If the latter, it is asserted that God the Father not only used Christ, but also was in Him in the unique union that characterized the incarnation. Both ideas are true and clearly taught elsewhere in Scripture.

Stated negatively, God's reconciling of the world involved "not counting their trespasses against them." God could act in this way because He placed those sins on Christ instead (5:21; Isa. 53:6). In actual performance, therefore, God through Christ was involving Himself in the work of reconciling sinners, not the task of condemning them (cf. John 3:17, "For

God did not send the Son into the world to judge the world; but that the world should be saved through Him."). The announcement of this tremendous act of grace on God's part had been committed to Paul and the other apostles, and in a sense to every believer, in the Great Commission.

VERSE 20. Because of this astounding message, Paul and his companions were motivated to see themselves as ambassadors for the absent Christ. An ambassador is an official representative, but he is more than just an errand boy. He represents the king or government. So Paul regarded his responsibility as a most solemn and honorable one. When he proclaimed the gospel, it was as though God Himself were speaking.

"We implore you on Christ's behalf" (NIV). As God was in Christ accomplishing the grounds of reconciliation, so in a roughly analogous way Paul suggested that God was in him and others (now that Christ was absent) issuing the appeal to men to accept by faith what God had done.[13] The objective aspects of reconciliation were accomplished by Christ; the subjective aspect requires man's response for salvation to be received.[14] This is not synergistic, however, for the biblical explanation indicates that even this turning to God is not man's work unaided (Jer. 31:8; John 6:44, 65).

VERSE 21. Here is the essence of what the gospel is all about. God the Father made Jesus, who was not unwilling in any sense and who was absolutely sinless, to be "sin" for us. It must be noted that God did not make Him a sinner (God does not make anyone a sinner), for then it would not be true that Christ "knew no sin." What is meant by the general term "sin" is all that is involved—its guilt, penalty, and shame. By imputing this to Christ, God could avoid imputing it to sinners. This cleared the way for God to impute His righteousness to us, a righteousness that is perfect and insures our approval with God. The gospel is the stupendous announcement that man's sin has been fully paid by Christ, and that God's righteousness is ours for the taking.

No wonder Paul was motivated to serve God without despairing. He was

13. It is not suggested that every feature of the union of the Father and the Son was present in Paul.

14. Lewis Sperry Chafer, *Systematic Theology,* III, 91-93.

gripped by the truth of what God had done for him in Christ, and he felt honored beyond words to be His ambassador.

Questions for Discussion

1. What is the condition of the believer between death and resurrection?
2. What is the biblical evidence for an intermediate body?
3. What kind of judgment will occur at the judgment seat of Christ?
4. In what sense did God reconcile the world to Himself?
5. What are the two aspects of the biblical teaching about reconciliation?

6

The Hardships of the Ministry

II Corinthians 6:1—7:1

A paradox of the Christian ministry is the coupling of sublime satisfaction and joy with almost unbelievable hardships in the lives of many Christian workers. Joining forces with God in the most worthy of enterprises is no guarantee that only ease and tranquillity will follow. The apostle Paul experienced just such contradictory circumstances, and the way he responded can be highly instructive for other Christians.

Paul had already faced a great variety of hardships in his ministry. He had found that not everyone had reacted favorably to the gospel. It is possible to "receive the grace of God in vain" (6:1). This poor response can discourage a minister who is not prepared for it. A poor response to the proclamation of the grace of God can take the form of rejecting the gospel outright, or of complaining against some of its implications for Christian living. Paul knew both kinds of response very well. He also had faced hardships from trials caused by non-Christians, and from being undermined or betrayed by people within the church. Those who serve God by ministering to others quickly learn that difficult experiences are frequent.

As Paul continued describing the character of his ministry, he pointed out this remarkable feature and urged his readers not to complicate the problem by their own responses.

7. Service to God involved great hardship (6:1-10)

a. Admonition to receive this ministry (6:1-2)

VERSE 1. Before giving a list of hardships which had characterized his ministry, Paul first exhorted his readers about their response. The fact that such an exhortation was necessary was itself one of the hardships of the ministry, for disappointment over negative or halfhearted compliance is a great burden to God's servants.

This admonition is based on the truths explained in 5:17-21. God in Christ had dealt with sin and made salvation possible. Furthermore, He had chosen Paul and others as ambassadors to convey the news of this outstanding grace of God to mankind everywhere. Thus Paul regarded himself and his associates as ones "working together with Him." The original text does not include the words "with Him,"[1] and one may question whether the thought is "working together with Him" or "working together with you Corinthians." The context (especially 5:20) clearly suggests the former, and this is reinforced by the similar Pauline expression, "we are labourers together with God" (I Cor. 3:9, KJV).[2]

Building on the fact that he was God's fellow worker in proclaiming reconciliation, Paul added the warning that his readers should not receive God's grace in vain. He was concerned lest any true believers, ones who had received the saving grace of God, should falter in their Christian lives, and at the judgment seat of Christ would be found empty (cf. 5:10). There was also the possibility that some readers might have made a superficial acceptance of the gospel, as illustrated by the varying responses in the parable of the sower (Matt. 13:3-9, 18-23), and would someday find it of no value. James also spoke of the Christian responsibility to "receive . . . the implanted word" (James 1:21, ASV). Failure to do this means stunted lives, spiritual powerlessness, and a reason for deep concern to God's servants.

1. Greek: *sunergountes* ("working together").
2. Greek: *theou gar esmen sunergoi*. This expression differs slightly, however, from that in 6:1, and may mean that Paul and Apollos were coworkers with each other, and both belonged to God. James L. Boyer, *For a World Like Ours*, p. 47, n. 1.

VERSE 2. A quotation of Isaiah 49:8 reinforced the apostle's point. The words were originally a statement of God to His servant the Messiah, in which the help of the Father was promised to Messiah for His salvation ministry. Inasmuch as Paul regarded Christian ministry as a "working together with Him," he understood that this fact of divine aid was a characteristic of proclaiming the gospel and highlighted the seriousness of his mission. To take lightly the grace of God is to assume enormous risk.

Emphasizing the phrases "acceptable time" and "day of salvation," Paul pointed out that the time was "now." Isaiah's prophecy had come to pass with the coming of Christ. As Christ's ambassador, commissioned by Him and ordered to proclaim the good news of salvation, Paul understood that the power of God was energizing his message, providing the help that had been promised to Christ centuries before.

b. Hardships encountered in performing this ministry (6:3-10)

VERSE 3. At the same time it was also the deep concern of Paul and his party that their lives should never bring reproach on the ministry of the gospel. Paul knew perfectly well that the truth of the gospel depended on what God had done, not on the persuasiveness of the preacher or the attractiveness of his life. Nevertheless, he was also aware that an inappropriate lifestyle could discredit the gospel in the eyes of an observing world. How often has the progress of the gospel been severely hindered by lack of integrity on the part of its ministers.

VERSE 4. In this verse and the next Paul stated a comprehensive term followed by nine descriptions, in groups of three, which characterized his experience as Christ's minister. This should have demonstrated to any honest inquirer what a minister should be.[3]

"In much endurance" (*en hupomonēi pollēi*) introduces the series. It is the only phrase which uses an accompanying adjective, and the only one with a term in the singular, thus suggesting that it is set apart from the

3. In the Greek text "ministers of God" is a nominative expression. Hence the rendering should be, "but as ministers of God, in everything commending ourselves."

others. Most likely it was intended as a broad introductory description, with the following phrases giving illustrations of the endurance which Paul and his company had displayed. The first three plural terms describe general types of situations where patient endurance was called for. "Afflictions" are various troubles which beset God's faithful servant. The term "necessities" (KJV; "hardships," NASB, NIV) refers to the strong demands or pressures on the minister if he is to perform as he should. "Distresses" are the frustrating situations in which God's servant feels hemmed in, and yet his ministry will not allow him to turn away.

VERSE 5. The next three terms are more specific than the preceding ones and describe situations in which the apostle was afflicted by others. "Beatings" (NASB; "stripes," KJV) had been administered to him five times by the Jews (11:24) and three times by Gentiles (11:25), including the episode at Philippi (Acts 16:23). "Imprisonments" (the term is plural, *phulakais*) had occurred at Philippi (Acts 16:23) and apparently at other places, although the New Testament records no other such incident prior to the time this epistle was written. It is possible, however, that Paul's appearance before the court of Gallio at Corinth had been preceded by an arrest and brief jailing (Acts 18:12). "Tumults" (riots) had occurred at Damascus, Jerusalem, Pisidian Antioch, Iconium, Lystra, Thessalonica, Berea, Corinth, and Ephesus thus far in Paul's ministry, and there would be many others before his career was through.

The next three terms denote what Paul voluntarily took on himself. "Labors" (NASB; "hard work," NIV) were the untiring efforts Paul put forth in carrying out his ministry for Christ. "Sleeplessness" was the consequence of his devotion to duty. This term probably refers not so much to insomnia as to his willingness to forego sleep in order to labor effectively. At Corinth he had labored at his tentmaking trade and carried on a spiritual ministry in addition. "Fastings" (KJV; "hunger," NASB, NIV) probably refer not to formal religious fasts, but to his doing without food at times in order to minister. When he had supported himself so the Corinthians would not have to pay him (11:9), he may well have decided to skimp on some meals. To restrict this reference to a voluntary action, rather than involuntary hunger, is supported by the fact that the term used here (*nēsteiais*) is distinguished by Paul from hunger and thirst (*limōi kai dipsei*) in 11:27.

VERSE 6. The following terms describe positively what Paul was and what every good minister should be. The first four items use single nouns. "Purity" denotes not only chastity but also an absence of anything blameworthy in deeds or motives. "Knowledge" conveys the thought that Paul's comprehension of God's truth was proper. He had a clear understanding of the gospel and its saving message. Purity of life alone would not have been sufficient if his knowledge of God's revelation were inadequate.

"Longsuffering" (KJV) or "patience" (*makrothumiāi*) is that quality which enables one to avoid retaliation when he is opposed. It is a trait that is usually exercised in relation to other persons, requiring its possessor to restrain himself from lashing out against whoever and whatever displeases him. Paul had great need for this quality in his relationship with the Corinthians. "Kindness" is goodness put into action. It is linked with "longsuffering" (KJV) in Galatians 5:22 and also in I Corinthians 13:4 (a cognate). Long-suffering withholds retaliation; kindness performs acts of goodness.

The next four expressions use pairs of words with the preposition instead of single terms. "In the Holy Spirit" (*en pneumati hagiōi*) puzzles some interpreters by its inclusion among the others in this list,[4] and they suggest a translation such as "in a holy spirit." However, when one realizes that this phrase is not simply buried in a long list but is the first in a new subseries using pairs of words, its position is not so startling. The Holy Spirit, who dwells in believers, produces spiritual fruit in their lives and empowers them for effective service. He had clearly demonstrated His presence in Paul's ministry.

"Love unfeigned" (KJV; Greek: *agapēi anupokritōi*) is that concern for others which is genuine and sincere, without any sham or pretense, and which seeks only the good of those to whom it is directed. All Christian

4. Alfred Plummer, *Corinthians Two*, pp. 196-197; C. K. Barrett, *The Second Epistle to the Corinthians*, pp. 186-187; Murray J. Harris, "2 Corinthians," *The Expositor's Bible Commentary*, X, 357.

ministry must be done with such a love in order for it to be effective
(I Cor. 13).

VERSE 7. Paul's ministry was also "in the word of truth" (*en logōi
alētheias*). Although some scholars understand the expression simply as a
claim to "truthful speech" (NIV), it is more characteristic of Paul[5] and the
New Testament generally[6] to see here a reference to God's revealed word
which never misleads men. It was this message from God which was the
basis for all of Paul's ministry.

"The power of God" is that divine energizing which lifts the labors of the
ministry above mere human effort. This power can turn human preaching
into a life-transforming force, and take simple words and use them to
convey eternal life (I Cor. 1:18-21).

"By the weapons of righteousness" describes Paul's ministry as carried
out with instruments that were proper. "Righteousness" can refer to that
imputed righteousness (that is, justification) which God has granted
believers and which provides the full panoply of spiritual armor for every
sort of struggle. Or it can denote the quality of the weapons that Christ's
servants must use. We are to present ourselves to God as "instruments of
righteousness" rather than of unrighteousness (Rom. 6:13). Both are true,
for the weapons of God's servants come from a righteous source and thus
are righteous in character. "For the right hand and the left" implies that
spiritual weapons are adequate for protection on all sides. Perhaps Paul was
also thinking in terms of the soldier, whose right hand held the sword and
the left the shield. Offensively and defensively God's servant is properly
armed to stand firm and emerge with ultimate victory in the battle against
spiritual foes.

VERSE 8. Paul here began a series of antitheses or paradoxes describing
himself and other faithful servants of God. "By glory and dishonor" states
the sort of treatment meted out to him. The Corinthians knew much better
than we how Paul had been treated at Corinth. One of the meanings of
"glory" (*doxēs*) was "favorable opinion or popularity," and this is probably

5. Ephesians 1:13; Colossians 1:5; II Timothy 2:15.
6. John 17:17; James 1:18.

the sense to be understood here. Some people had a high opinion of Paul and his helpers; others evaluated them as nothing and treated them accordingly.

"By evil report and good report" adds the information that some people mistreated Paul and his associates and gossiped about them. Some people maliciously spread false information about the apostle (Rom. 3:8; I Cor. 4:13), but others told the truth about him. Conflicting stories served to confuse those unacquainted with the truth, and added to the hardships of his ministry.

"As deceivers and yet true." Paul was frequently accused of concealing the truth in order to be popular (Gal. 1:10). Even today there are those who accuse Paul of teaching contrary to Jesus, and thus of being a deceiver. Yet those who understand his teachings have found him to be a true spokesman for God—Christ's apostle in every way.

VERSE 9. "As unknown, and yet well known" (KJV). Paul's foes often discounted him (I Cor. 4:3; II Cor. 13:3). He had not been a disciple of Jesus. Yet while some people minimized his authority, others acknowledged who he was. Most important, God knew him and that was what counted. But there were also hundreds of others blessed by his ministry, and they have multiplied into millions in the centuries since. These revere his memory and thank God for his ministry.

"As dying yet behold, we live." In view of their hardships and persecutions Paul and his party appeared to be living on borrowed time. Paul bore the marks of impending death in his body and in his mind (1:8-10; 4:10-11, 16). Yet God was preserving him so that he continued to live and minister.

"As punished yet not put to death." Paul was often beaten during his ministry, but God had spared his life (Acts 14:19-20; 16:22-23). Some people may have uncharitably implied that Paul's sufferings were a chastising from God because of personal sins. To Paul, however, they were an evidence of God's preserving power to enable his ministry to go forward.

VERSE 10. "As sorrowful yet always rejoicing." Another paradox of the Christian ministry is the fact of repeated occasions of sadness at the disappointing response so frequently encountered, coupled with an abiding joy that cannot be obliterated by circumstances. In Paul's case some of those times of sorrow had been caused by the Corinthians (2:3-4). Yet he always retained the inner joy supplied by the Holy Spirit (Gal. 5:22) which looked beyond the immediate stress to the ultimate victory and to the underlying rightness of his cause as an ambassador of Christ (5:20).

"As poor yet making many rich." The term "poor" (*ptōchoi*) denotes complete destitution which forces one to beg, in contrast to its synonyms which imply only lack of property.[7] Paul and his associates were regarded as poverty-stricken, often reduced to dependence on others for contributions. Yet the gospel they proclaimed was a treasure of incalculable worth, and those who responded in faith obtained spiritual wealth beyond human estimation.

"As having nothing and yet possessing all things." The previous phrase described Christ's servants in relation to others—making others spiritually rich in spite of no material resources. This phrase considers the situation from the servant's own standpoint. Paul and his party possessed little of this world's goods. Yet as Christians they did not fret over this circumstance, but recognized that although they no longer possessed even themselves, it was because Christ had bought them (I Cor. 6:20). This was no loss but rather great gain, for Christ had not merely bought them but also has joined all believers to Himself in a life-sharing union so that "all things are yours" (I Cor. 3:21-23, NIV).

C. An Appeal for Separation from Sin and Full Reconciliation to Paul (6:11—7:16)

1. An appeal that the Corinthians open their affections to Paul (6:11-13)

VERSE 11. As Paul described seven characteristics of his ministry in considerable detail (2:14—6:10), he had a clear purpose in mind. He desired a warm response from the Corinthians. Calling them by name, "O Corinthians," indicated the strong emotion he felt at this moment.[8] He had

---

7. Friedrich Hauck, "Ptōchos," TDNT, VI, 886-887.

8. On only two other occasions did Paul do this: to the Galatians, when their threatened

spoken freely to them, with unusual openness and without restraint (literally, "our mouth has opened to you"). The reason he had spoken so freely was because his "heart [had been] enlarged" (KJV). He had not turned away from them in petulance or disgust because of their recent opposition and mistreatment.

VERSE 12. Whatever problem still remained between the Corinthians and Paul was due to their attitude, not Paul's. The verb *stenochōreisthe,* translated as "straitened" (KJV) or "restrained" (NASB), conveys the idea of narrowness. Paul had just explained that his heart was opened wide toward them. There was no narrowness, no choking off of concern, no lack of sympathy on his part. It was the Corinthians themselves who were being hardhearted and restrained in their feelings toward Paul.

VERSE 13. It was only a "fair exchange" (NIV), therefore, that the Corinthians should open their hearts to Paul just as he had to them. After all, it is only proper that a mutual affection be displayed between children and their parents, and Paul could entreat them as children because he was their spiritual father (I Cor. 4:15).

2. An exhortation to separate from unbelievers and
   from sin (6:14—7:1)

Some interpreters have concluded that this section is out of place. The connection between 6:13 and 6:14 is regarded as forced, whereas 7:2 fits easily with 6:13. However, digressions are frequent with Paul, and a reason for this one is not difficult to find. The exhortation that the Corinthians open their hearts to Paul (6:13) must not be misunderstood as though he were asking for an undiscerning love that had no standards and no convictions. To return to Paul in a meaningful way would require a disavowal of all that was contradictory.

VERSE 14. "You must not get into double harness with unbelievers" is Barrett's felicitous rendering.[9] Paul's thought was undoubtedly based on

---

defection deeply disturbed him (Gal. 3:1), and to the Philippians, in warm gratitude for their generosity (Phil. 4:15).

9. C. K. Barrett, *Second Epistle,* p. 192.

the Old Testament injunction against yoking together an ox and an ass (Deut. 22:10). He was warning his readers against forming the sort of binding relationships with unbelievers which would weaken their Christian standards or compromise their ability to maintain a consistent witness. Earlier he had explained to the Corinthians that Christian separation did not mean absolute isolation from unbelievers (I Cor. 5:9-10). He had even told Christian spouses to remain with their unsaved mates as long as possible (I Cor. 7:12-13). Perhaps some Christians had now gone to the other extreme by making few distinctions between themselves and the world.

Paul was enunciating a principle of separation without providing a list of specific applications. From his writings, however, instances of this principle can be seen in the injunctions against marriage with an unbeliever (I Cor. 7:39), involving non-Christians in lawsuits between Christians (I Cor. 6:1-8), and eating meat in a pagan temple (I Cor. 8:10).[10]

By a series of questions the incongruity of such unequal yoking is illustrated. Righteousness and lawlessness cannot be in partnership. If one is to exist, the other must go. The same is true with light and darkness. In the spiritual realm light must dispel darkness; the two cannot coexist.

VERSE 15. Paul had just questioned the compatibility of the qualities of righteousness and lawlessness, and the realms from which they come, light and darkness. Next he contrasted the personal rulers of those realms, Christ and Belial, and asked what possible harmony they could have. In the Greek text here, Belial is actually "Beliar," apparently an alternate spelling.[11] This is its only occurrence in the New Testament. It is probably related to the Old Testament expression "sons of Belial," meaning "worthless persons," but in literature contemporary with the New Testament, the spelling "Beliar" was used as a name for the devil.[12] That is most certainly Paul's usage here.

10. Gordon D. Fee argues that the entire passage deals directly with the issue of eating in an idol's temple, although Fee admits that the absence in this context of any mention of food offered to idols is a weakness of his view. "II Corinthians VI.14—VII.1 and Food Offered to Idols," pp. 140-161.

11. It is not uncommon for the liquid letters *lambda* and *rho* to be interchanged.

12. Werner Foerster, "Beliar," TDNT, I, 607.

Fig. 7. Ruins of the Temple of Apollo at Corinth, one of many pagan shrines in the city.

Writing about individuals, Paul asked, "What has a believer in common with an unbeliever?" The literal translation is "what part" does he have, implying a common entity in which each party has a share. This is obviously impossible when believers belong to a different Lord, a different realm, and possess life of a different quality.

VERSE 16. The final question contrasts the sanctity of the temple of God to the temples of pagan idols. Although Greek and Roman pantheons had no difficulty in adding still another idol to their temple collections, such a concept is absolutely incongruous in the Judeo-Christian tradition. When Pilate, the Roman governor of Judea, brought his banners with the deified Caesar's likeness into the holy city of Jerusalem, horrified Jews regarded it as blasphemy.

How much more revolting should we regard it when Christians enter into unholy relationships with unbelievers, for "we are the temple of the living God." This is true corporately, as the succeeding quotations emphasize, for believers are made into a grand unity by the infusion of spiritual life which they all share. Thus they become a "spiritual house" (I Peter 2:5, NIV) and together are a "habitation of God" (Eph. 2:22, KJV). It is true corporately only because it is also true individually. Each Christian believer is himself a sanctuary where God dwells (I Cor. 6:19). Consequently, it is unthinkable that Christians should develop toleration for any sort of union that would bind them with unbelievers.

Paul reinforced this principle by a series of Old Testament quotations from different sources, cited somewhat freely, but all emphasizing the need for God's people to maintain separation from sin and from sinners.

"I will dwell in them and walk among them; And I will be their God, and they shall be My people." This is drawn from Leviticus 26:11-12, although the latter portion of the statement appears also in such passages as Hosea 2:23, Jeremiah 24:7, 30:22, 31:33, 32:38, and Ezekiel 37:27. The emphasis is on God's dwelling in believers as His sanctuary and thus acknowledging them as His own.

VERSE 17. "'Therefore, come out from their midst and be separate,' says the Lord. 'And do not touch what is unclean; And I will welcome you.'" This citation is based on a combination of Isaiah 52:11 and Ezekiel 20:34, 41. The words lay the responsibility on God's people to withdraw from unbelievers in order to be devoted to God.

VERSE 18. "'And I will be a Father to you, And you shall be sons and daughters to Me,' Says the Lord Almighty." The series of quotations ends with a weaving together of II Samuel 7:8, 14, Jeremiah 31:9, and Isaiah 43:6. These passages hold out the promise that God will act as a true Father to those sons and daughters who identify themselves with Him. But identification with God requires repudiation of unworthy associations which spiritually contaminate.

VERSE 1. Sensewise verse 1 belongs with the preceding material, basing its exhortation on the discussion just given. "Therefore" (*oun*) causes the reader to draw a logical inference from what has been said, and "these promises" are the ones given in 6:16b-18. Inasmuch as God is pleased to dwell among His people, to acknowledge them as His own, and promises to treat them as a father does his sons and daughters if they separate themselves from unbelievers and from sinful actions, then it follows that they should comply with the conditions which He has set down.

By calling his readers "beloved" as he does twice in the first epistle (10:14; 15:58) and twice in the second (7:1; 12:19), and by including himself in the exhortation ("let us"), Paul avoided an accusing tone and showed the openness of heart which he already mentioned in 6:11. "Flesh and spirit" are used here of the outward and inner aspects of the person. Although Paul often used "flesh" to refer to one's fallen nature and sinful appetites, he also used the term on some occasions to refer simply to one's outward being, as in 7:5 ("when we were come into Macedonia, our flesh had no rest," KJV). In this instance he meant that sinful defilement may contaminate both flesh, through the more obvious sins in the physical realm, and spirit, where thoughts and schemes may not be visible but where the deeper guilt falls.

Believers cleanse themselves from such defilement by repudiating these practices and "bringing holiness to completion in the fear of God" (literal). The process of progressive sanctification must be the experience of every believer. The same truth was stated in 3:18. The present participle "bringing to completion" (*epitelountes*) does not indicate that the process is ever completed in this life, but only that we must continually be engaged in that process. Attainment will occur at Christ's return when we see Him and become like Him (I John 3:2).

Questions for Discussion

1. What are some ways in which persons can receive the grace of God in vain?

2. What are some reasons why God allows His servants to undergo hardships?
3. What was Paul's attitude toward material wealth?
4. How far should one apply the command not to be bound together with unbelievers? What is meant by "bound"?
5. From whom should believers "separate," and for what reasons?

7

The Report from Titus

II Corinthians 7:2-16

"Hope deferred makes the heart sick, But desire fulfilled is a tree of life" (Prov. 13:12). Paul's hopes for the church at Corinth had received a terrible blow when his recent ministrations to it had been rejected. Yet a glimmer of hope still remained. Consequently, he had dispatched Titus to the Corinthians with a letter to make one more desperate effort to bring them back to holiness of life and reconciliation with Paul. In the meantime, he awaited the results, and it is always difficult to be patient in times of deep concern.

Paul had mentioned in 2:12-13 that he had left Ephesus in hopes of finding Titus, who would report on recent happenings in the problem-ridden church at Corinth. But while he waited at Troas, Titus did not appear. Therefore, Paul had left for Macedonia, still hoping to encounter Titus along the way. In fact, this is exactly what happened, as Paul will explain in 7:5-16. And the news was good! This encouraging development caused Paul to write II Corinthians, and accounted for the optimistic tone that permeates the letter, even when unpleasant matters are discussed. Because of this positive turn of events, Paul had good reason for appealing to his readers to open their hearts to him with the genuine warmth that had once characterized their relationship. Such an appeal prefaces his report of that happy reunion with Titus and his delight over the developments at Corinth.

3. A renewed appeal for openness toward Paul (7:2-4)

VERSE 2. "Make room for us" is an appropriate rendering of the Greek *chōrēsate hēmas.* Rather than joining with unbelievers and developing pagan associations, the Corinthians should be opening their hearts to Paul and others like him. The next three statements indicate why such an appeal was a reasonable one. Previous contacts with Paul and his party should have offered proof that there was nothing to fear at the hands of these messengers of God. The original word order emphasizes the absolute integrity of these men: "No one did we injure; no one did we corrupt; no one did we defraud." Do these statements imply that charges of this nature had been made, or at least that innuendoes of this sort had circulated at Corinth? If so, one could easily suppose that the denial of any injury inflicted could be in response to a charge that Paul had been overbearing in his dealings with them (1:23-24). The denial of his corrupting anyone could refer to Paul's having dealt with the case of incest in a wholesome, scriptural way which was intended to produce spiritual soundness (I Cor. 5:1-8). As to the absence of any fraud, perhaps some people had criticized the collection for the Christians at Jerusalem as a suspicious scheme from which the fundraisers themselves hoped to profit (I Cor. 16:1-4). Of course, these declarations are sufficiently general that they need not presuppose specific charges. Paul can be understood merely as ministering with such wholesomeness that the Corinthians' reception of him should be an easy and natural thing.

VERSE 3. Paul's intention was not to lay blame on the Corinthians. Much to the contrary, he was trying to win their allegiance once more. "I have spoken before" ties this passage to 6:11-13. This shows that Paul was aware of the digression in 6:14—7:1, and hence that it was not an interpolation by someone else but was part of the author's original discussion.

The depth of Paul's concern is indicated by his claim that the Corinthians were in his heart "to die together and to live together." The meaning is that they were so much on his heart that if he should die, it would be with their concerns in mind, and if he should go on living, it would be to serve their interests. Another aspect of his thought might have been that he and the Corinthians were joined with each other through faith in Christ, so that he expected to be resurrected along with them and go on living in eternal bliss with Christ and other believers (4:14). The mention of dying before living suggests such an explanation.

VERSE 4. The apostle was now able to say, "Great is my confidence in you, great is my boasting on your behalf," because he had received favorable news about the Corinthians from Titus (7:6-7). No longer must he tremble with uncertainty regarding them. Now he could say, "I am filled with comfort," the comfort which Titus' good report had brought. Even this statement could not do justice to the tremendous boost his spirit had received from this good news, so he added the exuberant claim, "I am overflowing with joy in all our affliction." The importance of the Corinthians occupied so large a place in Paul's thinking that good news regarding their response to the troublesome issues Paul had dealt with caused him to rejoice even in otherwise trying circumstances. Could his readers doubt that they found a genuine place in Paul's heart? Now if they will only reciprocate by showing as sympathetic a concern for Paul and his ministry.

4. The report from Titus (7:5-16)

a. Paul's meeting with Titus (7:5-7)

VERSE 5. Paul resumed the account of his search for Titus and their eventual meeting. He had begun this discussion earlier (2:12-13), but had interrupted it with an extended account of the character of his ministry (2:14—6:10), followed by a fervent appeal for the Corinthians to separate themselves from sin and be fully reconciled to him.

Mentioning again his trip into Macedonia, Paul explained the tremendous concern that had troubled his party at that time. They had not found Titus as expected in Troas (2:12-13), and had pressed on to Macedonia. The writer of Acts (20:1-2) gives no hint of these troubles (perhaps because he was not a participant at this time),[1] but they were very real to the traveling

---

1. The previous "we" section in Acts ended at Philippi (16:17), and the next one does not begin until 20:5. The presumption is that the author, Luke, was personally present only on those occasions when the first person "we" is used in Acts.

missionaries. "Our flesh had no rest" (KJV) is similar to "no rest for my spirit" (2:13), and describes the human realm in which sufferings occur. "Conflicts without" were the oppositions to the gospel and to the nurturing of converts which come from opponents both inside and outside the church. "Fears within" were the anxieties Paul experienced as he felt deep concern for his converts, and especially the Corinthians, not knowing how they had responded to his severe letter.

VERSE 6. Somewhere in Macedonia Paul met Titus and learned encouraging news about the Corinthians. Four times in this verse and the next Paul uses the word family "encourage" or "comfort" (*parakaleō, paraklēsis*) to stress the nature of the whole episode. First, he designated God as the encourager: "God who comforts the depressed, comforted us." This idea was previously expressed in 1:4-7, where the same word family appeared nine times in that statement. It was God who had stood beside these discouraged and apprehensive missionaries and provided the strength and comfort they needed to move forward with their ministry.

In saying that God encourages the downcast, Paul used a term that is usually translated "lowly" or "humble" (*tapeinous*). It denoted a low position, whether of social status or emotional state. Here the use summarizes what Paul had just stated about the condition of the missionaries who were beset by outward opposition and inward fears (7:5). Consequently, a translation such as "downcast," "downhearted," or "depressed" is indicated.

Paul next explained the factors which provided this encouragement. Foremost was the coming of Titus. The term "coming" also conveys the idea of "presence" (*parousiai*), and is frequently used of Christ's return to be present bodily with His saints. The arrival of Titus put to rest Paul's fears about the safety of his associate, and provided joy at the opportunity of reunion with this dear friend. He may have suspected that some calamity had befallen Titus since his arrival was delayed (2:13).

VERSE 7. A second factor that brought relief to Paul was the way the Corinthians had received Titus. "The comfort with which he was comforted in you" was equally important to Paul as Titus' safe arrival. The severe letter which Titus had taken to Corinth could have been misunderstood and followed by shabby treatment of the man who delivered it (2:4, 9; 7:15).

Fig. 8. Ruins of agora at ancient Corinth.

The third factor that encouraged the apostle was the report from Titus about the Corinthians' change of attitude toward Paul. The positive response to the severe letter was doubtless due in considerable measure to the tactful and effective way in which Titus had presented it. He had been the right person to send. As he rejoined Paul, he announced the Corinthians' "longing," probably their longing to see Paul after their change of heart and this period of estrangement. Their "mourning" was doubtless their deep sorrow over the sins which they had tolerated in their midst, but which Paul's rebuke had finally enabled them to view in proper light. Perhaps it also included sincere regret over their past mistreatment of Paul. "Your zeal for me" was the Corinthians' eager desire to rectify matters as Paul had instructed, and to become zealous supporters of the apostle rather than enamored with less worthy teachers (2:17). The nature of this report made him rejoice even more than merely being reunited with Titus. God had brought success to their efforts in strengthening the church.

b. The severe letter (7:8-13a)

VERSE 8. The relief which Paul felt over the success of his recent efforts to help the Corinthians prompted him to discuss the severe letter which had worried him after he had sent it. Some interpreters identify this letter as I Corinthians; however, the view adopted in this commentary explains the severe letter as one no longer extant but written by Paul subsequent to I Corinthians and following a "painful visit" to Corinth not mentioned in Acts (see Introduction, "Background"; also 2:1-4).

Paul recognized that he had caused the Corinthians sorrow by the severe letter. Yet there was no way he could have dealt effectively with the problems at Corinth without raising painful issues and speaking forthrightly about offences. "I do not regret it; though I did regret it." He had no regrets about what he had written, although there was a time (before he knew the outcome) when he had serious misgivings about sending it.[2] The report from Titus confirmed the fact that the letter had indeed grieved the Corinthians, but only for a brief time.[3] Happily it produced the desired results.

VERSE 9. Now Paul could rejoice, not because the Corinthians had been caused some temporary sorrow, but because their distress produced a change of heart toward the problem. They had been grieved "according to God" (kata theon), that is, in accordance with God's will. Theirs had been a distress produced by godly conviction, and it had proceeded along lines that God intended.

As a result the Corinthians had not been damaged in any way by Paul's

---

2. It is easier to imagine such regret over the sending of a noncanonical severe letter than to suppose the apostle regretted sending I Corinthians, which he knew was inspired (I Cor. 2:7, 13; 14:37). It is more difficult to decide what portions of I Corinthians Paul would have wished he had not said.

3. Literally, "for an hour" (pros hōran). This is the same expression used in Galatians 2:5 and Philemon 15, denoting in both instances a comparatively short time, but in the latter case a period of some months.

severe letter. Because they had allowed the letter to produce these godly effects, they avoided any injury which the harshness of tone might otherwise have caused.

VERSE 10. There is a great contrast between the two kinds of sorrow Paul was talking about. The sorrow which is prompted by understanding the will of God is not an end in itself, but produces repentance unto salvation. This repentance is a true change of mind (*metanoian*) regarding the matters at issue, not just a response of emotion. Unbelievers who are brought to this kind of repentance experience the salvation of God. Sinning Christians, when convicted of their sin and genuinely repentant, will resume the sort of conduct that should characterize their salvation in its present aspect. The adjective *ametameleton* ("without regret, not to be repented of") should be taken with "repentance" or "repentance unto salvation," but not with "salvation" alone, inasmuch as this last would state a truism that is hardly necessary.[4] The thought is that those who repent in this true way never regret it.

The sorrow of the world, however, ultimately produces death. Mere grief which is not brought about by godly conviction and therefore does not issue in true repentance and spiritual transformation brings only remorse, bitterness, and despair. Being unconditioned by spiritual factors, it leaves the person unchanged in his relation to God and his situation only becomes worse. It is a harbinger of that final disillusionment of the sinner, death itself. Lenski expressed it well: "The world's grief is already death's shadow closing down."[5] A prime example in the New Testament is Judas, whose bitter grief led him not to faith but to suicide (Matt. 27:3-5).

VERSE 11. Paul pointed to the various effects which the Corinthians' sorrow had produced in them, thereby demonstrating that theirs was a godly sorrow. "Earnestness" (*spouden*) refers to the diligence and eagerness with which they now had devoted themselves to dealing with the issues Paul

4. Philip E. Hughes, however, refers the thought to Paul as having no regret for having caused this kind of grief (7:8). *Commentary on the Second Epistle to the Corinthians*, pp. 271-272.

5. R. C. H. Lenski, *Interpretation of First and Second Corinthians*, p. 1110.

had addressed. "Vindication"[6] (*apologian*) was the effort to clear themselves of guilt when Paul's rebuke had come. "Indignation" (*aganaktēsin*)
was their outrage over the sin in their midst and the particular offender.
"Fear" (*phobon*) was their fear of God's displeasure, and perhaps also their
respect for Paul's sternness and his possible coming in wrath (I Cor. 4:21;
II Cor. 13:2). "Longing" (*epipothēsin*) denoted their yearning to see the
matter rectified and good relations with Paul restored. "Zeal" (*zēlon*)
described the Corinthians' enthusiasm for getting the matter settled soon
before Paul came. Punishment (*ekdikēsin;* "avenging of wrong," NASB) of
the offender would carry this whole matter through to the appropriate
conclusion.

This conduct of the Corinthians, resulting from Paul's letter to them and
aided by the ministry of Titus in their midst, showed them to be without
fault in their present dealing with the matter. When Paul said that they had
showed themselves to be "clear" (KJV) or "innocent" (NASB, NIV) did he
mean that they as a church had been innocent all along of any complicity
in the offense being discussed, and that their only fault was their negli-
gence in dealing with the wrong that an individual had committed?[7]
Although this view fits well with 7:12, where a single offender is mentioned, it has more difficulty providing a natural explanation for the
mourning and repentance that the whole congregation exhibited (7:7, 9).
The more common explanation regards the statement as expressing that
they had cleared themselves by their wholesome and positive response to
Titus and the severe letter.[8] The term "innocent" (*hagnous*) need not imply
that the readers had never erred in their relation to the problem. The
statement can simply mean that since their repentance, they had shown
themselves to be without fault.

VERSE 12. Here Paul used a common Hebrew manner of expression,
choosing the chief reason for his action and stating it in a way that seems to

6. Each succeeding term in this list is introduced with the adversative *alla* ("but"), so that
the full expression should be understood as follows: "[not only this] but vindication, [not only
this] but indignation. . . ."

7. This is the explanation of C. K. Barrett, *The Second Epistle to the Corinthians,* p. 212.

8. Alfred Plummer, *Corinthians Two,* p. 223.

deny other reasons. This dramatic form of statement is found in such passages as Hosea 6:6 (NIV): "For I desire mercy, not sacrifice" (in reality God desired both). Certainly Paul was not saying that he did not have the offender in mind when he wrote. His point was, however, that the real aim of his severe letter went far beyond a few individuals.

Our knowledge of the details prompting this letter is admittedly meager, and thus we can only suggest possibilities. The view espoused in this commentary sees the offender as the ringleader of opposition against Paul (and perhaps Titus). The one offended was probably Paul, or perhaps Titus, but this is less likely.[9] With this understanding, Paul is regarded as saying that his primary concern was not to secure punishment for the offender or vindication for himself. What he really wanted was for the Corinthians to prove to themselves that their response to spiritual truth and to God's messengers was right.[10] To accede to the directives of the apostle would rectify the situation, true repentance and an altered course of action would bring God's approval, and this in turn would remind the Corinthians of the importance of heeding the instruction of Christ's duly chosen apostles.

VERSE 13a. Consequently, the report of Titus had encouraged Paul and his companions. The wisdom of the course of action Paul had taken was vindicated.

c. The joy of Titus (7:13b-16)

VERSE 13b. An additional blessing occurred for Paul when he saw the high spirits of Titus at his return. Titus' reception at Corinth had refreshed his spirit. It had been a confirmation of the good things Paul had told him about the church in spite of its recent problems.

In all likelihood Titus had undertaken this trip to Corinth with considerable trepidation. His feelings may have been similar to those of Timothy on an earlier occasion when Paul had to urge the Corinthians not to

9. The other view identifies the offender as the incestuous man of I Corinthians 5, and regards the one offended as the man's aggrieved father.

10. The King James Version has followed manuscripts which transposed "your" and "our" (humōn . . . hēmōn), a common scribal error. This results in alteration of the sense, making it Paul's concern for the Corinthians, rather than their concern for him.

intimidate him if he came (I Cor. 16:10-11). In the case of Titus, the wholesome reaction of the Corinthians to him greatly eased his mind, and brought him a spiritual refreshment which was not just momentary but was still present at the time the epistle was written.[11]

VERSE 14. "If in anything I have boasted to him about you" implies that Paul had recounted to Titus some of the good points of the Corinthians. Paul was a missionary statesman of sufficient stature to see beyond momentary lapses to the inherent value of these believers. He saw their potential and remembered their successes. Unpleasant incidents, even when they had been directed against him personally, could not blind him to the genuine greatness of this church in which outstanding spiritual victories had occurred.

Paul was gratified that the Corinthians had not disappointed him in their treatment of Titus. By the way they had received Titus, they had proved to Titus that Paul had not exaggerated their virtues. Once again Paul's veracity had been demonstrated, for he had always spoken truly to the Corinthians on his visits to them, and he had also spoken truth about them to others, even when some people might have found it hard to do so.

VERSE 15. Not only had Titus discovered that Paul had not misjudged the good qualities of the Corinthian believers, but he also continued to be emotionally stirred as he remembered their ready response to his ministry. Instead of receiving him with suspicion or hostility, they had been prepared to obey. In fact, they had received him "with fear and trembling." This phrase occurs three other times in the New Testament. It is used of Paul's own feelings when he first visited Corinth (I Cor. 2:3); of the proper attitude of Christian slaves toward their masters (Eph. 6:5); and of the way all believers should conduct their lives before God (Phil. 2:12). It need not depict a cringing and terrified panic, but rather a humble and respectful understanding of one's position. In the case of the Corinthians, they may have realized their problems before Titus arrived, and were in the proper frame of mind to respond obediently to the apostolic instructions which he would deliver.

11. The verb "has been refreshed" (*anapepautai*) is a perfect tense, indicating the present condition resulting from a past action.

VERSE 16. Thus the report of Titus brought joy to Paul's heart and renewed confidence that his faith in the Corinthians was not misplaced. The church at Corinth had its problems, but the important thing was that it had begun to deal with them in accordance with scriptural and apostolic directives. Paul would not need to hesitate in visiting them again. Nor did he have to give up hope of finding at Corinth a hearty response to the collection. He could discuss the matter of the collection in the next major section of the epistle.

Questions for Discussion

1. What is involved in genuine repentance?
2. What principles are important in dealing with individuals or groups that have displayed hostility?
3. What elements in Paul's character do you see displayed in this portion of the letter?
4. As you reflect on the first major section of II Corinthians, what were some of the characteristics of Paul's ministry that impressed you?

THE COLLECTION
FOR THE POOR CHRISTIANS
IN JERUSALEM

(II Corinthians 8–9)

8

The Collection
for the Jerusalem Christians

II Corinthians 8:1-15

Paul's raising of funds among the Gentile churches for the poverty-stricken Christians at Jerusalem formed an important part of his mission on his third journey. Early in the church's history the problem of economic need had arisen in Jerusalem. The first trouble within the infant church revolved around a charge of inequity in meeting the needs of Christian widows (Acts 6:1-7). A famine accentuated the privation that the persecuted Jerusalem church was doubtless already experiencing, and prompted the sister church at Antioch to hasten to her aid (Acts 11:27-30; 12:25). Paul had been one of the delegates from Antioch who delivered this assistance, and his interest in the material needs of the believers at Jerusalem continued during his ministry. He remarked in writing to the Galatians that he was eager to respond to the plea of the Jerusalem saints regarding the poor among them (Gal. 2:10).

This particular project of the collection had begun prior to the writing of II Corinthians. The earliest mention of it is in I Corinthians 16:1-4. In that reference Paul seems to have been responding to a communication he had received from the Corinthians, and one of their inquiries was concerning the collection. Paul's response indicated that the project was already underway in Galatia, and that the procedure involved offerings gathered each Sunday. Eventually, messengers chosen by the churches would transport the funds to Jerusalem.

In this epistle Paul urgēd the Corinthians to complete their fundraising, which had begun a year before (II Cor. 8:10). The various problems that had erupted in this church during the intervening time would certainly have had an adverse effect on the success of the collection. However, the issue had been resolved and Paul planned to visit them again. It was time to complete what they had started (II Cor. 8:6).

From Paul's epistle to the Romans, written after he had made the visit to Corinth (which was still in prospect as he wrote II Corinthians), we learn that the Corinthian church did complete the project. Paul told the Romans that Achaia (of which Corinth was the capital) as well as Macedonia had made a contribution (Rom. 15:25-27).

III. The Collection for the Poor Christians in Jerusalem (8:1—9:15)

A. The Contribution of the Macedonians (8:1-5)

VERSE 1. In beginning this rather lengthy discussion of the collection, Paul laid a foundation by giving a beautiful description of the Macedonian churches' response to the project. These were the churches at Philippi, Thessalonica, and Berea. At least, these were the churches of Macedonia which are mentioned in Acts. Whether others had been established by this time is not known.

The generous giving by the Macedonians was attributed not simply to an altruistic spirit or a warm-hearted concern, but to "the grace of God." Generous giving to the Lord's work is an evidence that God has been working in people's hearts. It was He who had moved the Macedonians to give. Paul left no room for personal pride. At the same time, this truth enabled Paul to refer to the exceptional giving in Macedonia without seeming to elevate those churches above the Corinthians. The credit really belonged to God's grace, not to superior responsiveness. Paul hoped the Corinthians would be receptive to the development of this divine grace in their lives.

VERSE 2. What made the contribution of the Macedonian churches so impressive were the circumstances out of which it was made. There had been a "great ordeal of affliction" in these churches. Reference to some of this persecution is found in I Thessalonians 1:6 and 2:14, as well as in Acts 17:6-9, 13. Nevertheless an abundance of joy, which opposition and suffering could not remove, was present in the Macedonians' hearts. This was all the more remarkable because the pressures imposed by deep poverty were also on them. Hated and attacked by outsiders, and constricted by serious economic needs, they did not allow any of this to deter them from giving a truly generous offering. They obviously had put the interests of others far above their own. The example of the widow's mite comes to mind (Mark 12:41-44). The depth of their poverty was far exceeded by the wealth of their generous spirit.

VERSE 3. Paul gave solemn testimony to the Macedonians' action: it was according to their ability, and in fact even beyond their ability. There is no hint here of an assessment or a fixed percentage imposed on them. More than that, their giving must have gone beyond normal prudence as they opened their hearts and their purses for the saints at Jerusalem. And their gift had been absolutely voluntary. Paul had not begged them to give at all.

VERSE 4. The truth of the matter was, the Macedonians had begged the missionary party for the privilege of giving! Even though the collection project had already begun in Galatia prior to Paul's arrival in Macedonia (I Cor. 16:1), he had apparently not begun promoting it in Macedonia. Perhaps he felt that the afflictions and the poverty that confronted those churches at that time would make it unwise to urge a campaign to raise funds for use elsewhere. The Macedonians might well have responded that someone should be raising funds to help them. When they became aware, however, of what other churches were doing, they began begging Paul "with much entreaty" that they be given the privilege of participating.

A very literal rendering of the phrase is: "begging of us the grace and the participation in the ministry to the saints."[1] Inasmuch as the word "grace" (*charis*) was used a few lines earlier to refer to God's bestowal of a generous spirit, it could easily be so understood here. The sense then is that the

---

1. Greek: *deomenoi hēmōn tēn charin kai tēn koinōnian tēs diakonias tēs eis tous hagious.*

Macedonians asked for the privilege to receive and display this gracious gift from God so they could participate in giving to the saints in Jerusalem. In spite of persecution and poverty, they did not want to miss any of the grace of God, including the grace of giving.

VERSE 5. The Macedonians, however, had responded with much more than money. They had first given themselves "to the Lord and to us." It is best to regard these phrases as referring to two aspects of the same thing, for the text does not say that the Macedonians *first* gave themselves to the Lord and *then* to the missionaries. As the Macedonians became sensitive to the will of God for their lives, they wholeheartedly dedicated themselves to Him, and this involved accepting the guidance of God's missionaries—the apostolic party. They had put themselves at God's disposal and had therefore submitted to His chosen leaders. This feature of the Macedonians' action was more impressive to Paul than the generous gift they had given, for it was the basis for their action. They had complied with God's messengers in this project of the collection because it was a part of their deeper dedication to God Himself.

Although this giving of themselves to God and His ministers referred to the Macedonian churches collectively, it is also true that some within those churches literally devoted themselves to Paul as his helpers in his ministry. Examples are Sopater (Berea); Jason, Aristarchus, and Secundus (Thessalonica); Epaphroditus (Philippi); and Gaius (somewhere in Macedonia).[2]

B. Encouragement to Similar Generosity in Corinth (8:6–15)

1. The challenge to complete the collection (8:6-12)

VERSE 6. "The same grace" (KJV) or "this gracious work" (NASB) is literally "this grace" (*tēn charin tautēn*), and refers to the collection as an evidence of God's gracious working in believers' hearts to produce this Christian virtue. Giving to the Lord's work and helping others in His family is a spiritual virtue that every believer can and should cultivate. One need

2. Acts 17:5-9; 19:29; 20:4; Philippians 2:25.

Fig. 9. Ruins of shops along Lechaion Street in ancient Corinth.

not be wealthy, as is obvious from the example of the Macedonians. Giving of oneself to God makes the difference, for it changes one's perspective toward money and material things.

Paul now urged Titus to complete this project which he had begun in Corinth in the past. It is clear from other statements in the passage that Paul's urging[3] of Titus is to be understood as presently going on and with reference to a return visit to Corinth (8:16-24).

3. The aorist infinitive *parakalesai* is used here in the common epistolary sense.

Identification of the time when Titus had previously initiated the collection project is less certain. If we are to understand that Titus was the first person to announce the project at Corinth, then he must have made a visit prior to the writing of I Corinthians, inasmuch as the collection was already known in Corinth at that time (16:1-4). Perhaps Titus had delivered the lost letter (I Cor. 5:9), although we possess no information regarding the circumstances. A less likely explanation is that on Titus' recent mission to Corinth with the severe letter, he had begun the work of revitalizing the collection project which had faltered during the difficulties there.

VERSE 7. Because the Corinthians had excelled in so many spiritual virtues, Paul did not hesitate to urge that they respond in the collection project also. He named five of their exemplary spiritual qualities, and judging by these he felt confident that the Corinthians would rectify the lack of a similar excellence in the more mundane virtue of giving.

"Faith" included not only the Corinthians' initial faith in Christ's redemptive work, but also their continuing trust in Him for guidance, supply of needs, and strength for each day. "Utterance" (*logōi*) probably referred to their ability to give expression to their faith as they shared their faith with each other and with the unconverted. "Knowledge" was their understanding of spiritual truth, largely as the result of the excellent teachers who had ministered among them. "All diligence" (KJV) was the earnestness with which they had pursued their Christian lives. Theirs was no lackadaisical or perfunctory performance. Sometimes, it is true, their zeal had been misdirected, but it was often extremely wholesome, especially in recent weeks (II Cor. 7:11). "Your love to us" (KJV) is literally "the love among you which is from us."[4] The sense is, "the love which we inspired in you." These traits were admirable, and should be rounded out by a display of generosity that would clearly show that their Christian commitment was not without its practical side.

Some scholars have explained these spiritual graces as instances of the charismatic gifts described in I Corinthians 12:8-10.[5] This explanation fits

4. Greek: *tēi ex hēmōn en humin agapēi*. This reading is adopted by UBS and Nestle, although manuscript evidence gives several alternatives.

5. Philip E. Hughes, *Commentary on the Second Epistle to the Corinthians*, pp. 296-297.

well with several terms in that list; however, the references to earnestness and love are not special charismatic gifts from the Spirit but should characterize every fruitful Christian. Consequently, understanding the five characteristics in this statement in the other sense explained above seems preferable to this writer.

VERSE 8. Although Paul was an apostle, he was not issuing orders but was endeavoring to produce a spontaneous response. He felt that the level of spiritual understanding which these readers had, coupled with the revived warmth of their admiration for him, would prompt them to be motivated by the "earnestness of others" (NASB, NIV), that is, the example of the energetic Macedonians.

Laying this challenge before the Corinthians would provide an opportunity for them to prove the sincerity of their love. Merely ordering them to comply would test only their obedience. Challenging them by the example of other generous churches would test the depth of their own concern for the needy saints in Jerusalem.

VERSE 9. Paul had used the Macedonians as an illustration of Christian love and grace displayed toward others, but he next turned to the greatest example of all. It was the Lord Jesus Christ whose action on man's behalf showed what true grace means. It was He who was incomparably rich in His preexistence with the Father. Yet He did not shrink from laying aside that manner of existence in order to become a man.[6] In this sense "He became poor," which does not imply merely that His days on earth were not affluent. Paul referred to Christ's infinite condescension from the pre-existent to the incarnate state.

The purpose of Christ's great condescension was that men might become rich. By faith in Him and regeneration by the Spirit, believers have become immeasurably wealthy with spiritual position and blessings. The ultimate enjoyment of these riches in Christ awaits the age to come, but even now as sons of God and heirs of the promise to Abraham (Gal. 3:26, 29; 4:7) believers are possessors of a wealth far surpassing material riches. Inasmuch as this supreme example of giving oneself was provided by the

6. See Homer A. Kent, Jr., "Philippians," *The Expositor's Bible Commentary*, XI, 122-127.

very Lord whom believers profess to follow, and who has made them rich for eternity in the things which really matter, how could any Christian deliberately resist the Spirit of Christ who is working within the heart to make each believer more Christ-like? A self-sacrificing, generous spirit should be normal for every Christian.

VERSE 10. Paul then gave his opinion in the matter of the Corinthians and the collection. He issued no order but advised that it would be best for them to finish what they had started. He reminded them that a year ago they had begun to collect the funds. Furthermore, it had not been a grudging start, but a willing one.

Although some translations suggest that the Corinthians had begun the project *first,* presumably before the Macedonians (NASB, NIV), the verb "to begin beforehand" (*proenarchomai*)[7] simply conveys the thought that the beginning in question was before the present writing. Hence Paul was saying that the Corinthians had previously started; now they needed to finish.

VERSE 11. "But now finish doing it also" is stated as a command, but it must be understood merely as advice rather than as a strict order (8:10). The Corinthians' readiness to begin needed to be matched by an equal readiness to carry through with appropriate performance.

Paul then introduced the thought which will be elaborated in the next verse, that the Corinthians' contribution should be determined by the parameters of what they possessed (literally, "out of what one has"). He was not asking something unreasonable.

VERSE 12. The key to one's actions lies in one's attitude. If there is a genuine determination to participate, an appropriate action ought to proceed from that, and God will find such response acceptable. The principle Paul emphasized is that the attitude is the essential element, not the size of the gift.

The implications of Paul's instructions are obvious. One cannot legitimately excuse himself from participating in the funding of God's work because his gift may be small. God assesses what is done—not by the size of

7. Arndt, p. 712.

the total, but by the resources available to the giver. If one does not have sufficient to make a sizable gift, God does not expect him to do it. No gift is too small to "count" with God, if it proceeds from a willing heart and is appropriate to the resources out of which it is given. Scripture places more emphasis on the willingness of the giver than the size of the gift.

This passage also implies that a proper willingness will result in action. True willingness is not idle promises or casual desire. When accomplishment does not follow, it is usually because the willingness is not very strong. The will is shallow and ineffective, not committed enough to resist other attractions which divert attention from the original purpose.

At the same time a true willingness to become involved in the Lord's work will usually mean that one follows through with an appropriate gift. No amount or percentage was levied on these readers for this special offering, except that it should be "according to what a man has," rather than something beyond what he has. Yet this readiness to give implies a generous attitude of heart, and not a selfish and grudging donation that represents to the donor only a pittance.

2. The aim of equality (8:13–15)

VERSE 13. Paul may have anticipated a possible objection that the Corinthians were being asked to impoverish themselves so that others might be enriched. Thus he made it clear that he was not asking for the wealthy to become poor by exchanging places with them. That would merely shift the problem from one location to another. The "others" mentioned in this verse were the Jerusalem Christians who were presently deprived of necessities. Paul was urging the principle of equalization.

VERSE 14. At present the Corinthians were experiencing relative abundance in comparison with the less fortunate Jerusalem saints. By sharing with the Jerusalem Christians, their economic lack (which had occurred through no fault of their own) would be supplied.

This assistance would help restore the Christians at Jerusalem to a condition of better economic health so that they "may become a supply for your want" in the future should the situations be reversed. Although such a recovery is difficult to envision during these early decades in Jerusalem, one could not predict with certainty what might happen in specific cases, and the principle of equality is a reasonable one.

It should be obvious that Paul did not insist on a mechanical or legislated socialism. All Christians are not envisioned as being exactly the same economically as each other. It is assumed that some will be richer than others. Christian practice simply calls for those who have a surplus of necessities to share their bounty with those who lack.

Although Paul elsewhere used the argument that financial assistance sent to Jerusalem was a fair exchange for the spiritual benefits Jerusalem had shared with the Gentile churches, that does not seem to be his point here (Rom. 15:27). There is no good reason to suppose that he is using "abundance" (*perisseuma*) and "lack" (*husterēma*) in different senses in this comparison. It is best to explain the statement as referring to the possibility of an opportunity for Jerusalem to share its goods with the Corinthians.

VERSE 15. Paul summed up his appeal for a generous offering and his emphasis on the principle of equality by citing an Old Testament passage: "He who gathered much did not have too much, and he who gathered little had no lack" (Paul's paraphrase of Exodus 16:18). The historical reference is to the manna in the wilderness where this principle of equality was illustrated. Those who had collected the most were able to use only what they needed, and the excess rotted (Exod. 16:19-21). Those who gathered less found that it was sufficient. In both instances God's direct action is implied, in causing the excess to be destroyed and in making the smaller amounts cover the need.[8]

By analogy, Paul regarded material prosperity as God's provision for the Corinthians. Figuratively, prosperity was their manna. They should beware of selfishness or a tendency to hoarding, for God made it clear in the wilderness that He desired everyone's needs to be met. Thus whether it was

8. Another commentator sees the incident as nonmiraculous, whereby all in each tent who gathered the manna pooled their gathering and then measured out equitable quantities to each person. The excess simply spoiled by natural means, and the shortage was averted by sharing. Hughes, *Commentary,* pp. 307-308.

by miraculous means (as the manna for the Israelites), or by the production of spiritual graces in the lives of Christians (so that they will share with their needy brothers), God expects the needs of His children to be supplied. For a Christian to resist such an appeal for help is to raise questions about the genuineness of his commitment to Christ (James 2:14-17; I John 3:17).

Questions for Discussion

1. Why were the Jerusalem Christians poorer than others?
2. Why did Paul refer to giving as a grace?
3. List the reasons why one should give to the needs of others.
4. What are the differences between Paul's concept of equality and the philosophies of socialism and communism?
5. Why are Christian appeals for money sometimes resented? What safeguards should be followed?

9

The Importance of Generosity

II Corinthians 8:16—9:15

Most people have a strong attachment to their money. Selfishness is publicly deplored but privately practiced. In Christian circles the problem persists as much as elsewhere, for it is a human weakness that knows few exceptions.

For some people the problem is complicated because of a faulty attitude toward money. The biblical phrase "filthy lucre" (I Tim. 3:3, KJV) has been misunderstood as though it refers to every kind of money. In reality, the expression means "shameful gain," and refers to ill-gotten wealth, not to money that is honorably acquired. Money per se is neither good nor evil. It is merely the medium by which one's labors can be exchanged for services or goods. Money can be the cause of much that is good, provided that it is used for worthy purposes.

Sometimes Christians regard any talk about money or fundraising as unspiritual. Pastors frequently are hesitant to mention the need for funds to carry on appropriate ministries lest they be misunderstood. The well-publicized efforts of religious hucksters with questionable ethics and high-pressure tactics make some pastors afraid to discuss finances at all. In some circles, the claim "we never ask for money" is supposed to imply a deeper faith, even though the statement itself may be a kind of appeal.

Paul, however, was not hesitant in asking believers to give of their funds to assist the Lord's work and the Lord's needy people. He understood what money is and what it can accomplish. If it is proper to ask Christians to present themselves to Christ for His use (Rom. 12:1), then it is proper to ask them to present their funds.

From this collection, whereby Paul was endeavoring to raise a substantial offering for the needy Christians at Jerusalem, the modern reader can learn the importance of a right attitude toward money. The Christian is a steward of God's property. He must be sensitive to the wisest use of the goods with which he has been entrusted, and be aware of the needs of his fellow members in the body of Christ.

C. The Sending of Titus and His Companions
   ## (8:16—9:5)

1. Introduction of the messengers (8:16-24)

a. Titus (8:16-17)

VERSE 16. Paul sent three men to Corinth for the task of receiving the collection. The leader of this delegation was Titus. He had previously been mentioned in this letter (2:13; 7:6, 13, 14; 8:6), and was already well known to the Corinthians, for he had just come from Corinth with a report to Paul (7:7).

Although the apostle credited God with creating a concern for the Corinthians in the heart of Titus, Paul had been the instrument God had used to accomplish this. Paul had urged Titus to return to Corinth and complete the work of the collection (8:6). Paul was obviously pleased that his efforts had been successful and Titus was undertaking the work, but he understood that his attempt to persuade Titus might have failed if God had not produced in Titus a responsive heart.

How interesting that Titus' concern or earnestness was explained as "for you" (KJV), rather than for the Jerusalem saints. Neither Paul nor Titus was prompted solely by sympathy for those in physical need; each also desired to see a spirit of generosity displayed among the Corinthians. It would be an evidence of spiritual growth on their part, and such a prospect excited Paul and Titus.

VERSE 17. The evidence of what God had done in Titus could be seen in his response. He had accepted Paul's appeal to make the trip. Furthermore, he was enthusiastic about it. Paul's actual wording can be rendered, "very earnest," or, "more earnest [than others or than I]." To send a man back on an arduous and perhaps dangerous journey which he had just completed could have made Paul hesitate to ask. To send Titus back to a church that was just coming out of serious difficulty and then to ask him to handle the delicate task of fundraising among these Christians might have caused Paul to wonder whether Titus would take the job. He need not have worried. Titus was ready to go. In fact, his eagerness was such that he would have gone without Paul's urging. God had placed a yearning in Titus' heart so that his going[1] was as if it were "on his own initiative" (NIV).

b. The brother (8:18-21)

VERSE 18. The next member of this traveling delegation was designated simply as "the brother." If it seems strange to find him referred to in such an inexact manner, it must be remembered that there would have been no problem for the original readers. They would already have met him as one of the messengers delivering this epistle. If Titus were the one who first read this scroll to the congregation at Corinth, a simple gesture toward one of his companions would have made this man's identity clear.

This Christian brother is described as one whose praise in connection with the proclamation of the gospel was echoed throughout all the churches. Clearly he was a well-known and perhaps much-traveled Christian, whose untarnished reputation made him a wise choice for this particular mission.

Although no further data can be found for identifying this brother, attempts to identify him have been numerous.[2] The most frequently mentioned candidate is Luke. Unfortunately the chief reason suggested for this identification, that "his praise is in the gospel" (*New Scofield Reference Bible*) refers to the written Gospel of Luke, is clearly invalid. That

1. The verb "he went" (*exelthen*) is epistolary, referring to a present event which will be past by the time the addressees read it. "Has gone" or "is going" would be appropriate translations. Titus in all likelihood delivered II Corinthians.

2. An excellent resumé of views is given by Philip E. Hughes, *Commentary on the Second Epistle to the Corinthians,* pp. 312-316.

written Gospel was not in circulation by this time. To explain "the brother" as "his brother," meaning Titus' physical brother, would presumably require us to explain "our brother" (8:22) as Paul's brother—an explanation few scholars are prepared to adopt. At present we have no way to ascertain the identity of this brother, except to propose that he may have been one of those mentioned in Acts 20:4.[3]

The wisdom of Paul's action in sending several unimpeachable messengers should be obvious. By sending more than one, he protected the messengers from charges of misuse of funds.

VERSE 19. This "brother" was not only held in high regard by many churches, but also had been elected by them. The verb "chosen" (*cheirotonētheis*) originally meant "to elect by a vote of raised hands." This verb also connoted "to choose" or "to appoint," as the compound form in Acts 10:41 indicates. In this passage, the selection process seems to imply congregational action rather than administrative appointment. This is the way the Seven were chosen at Jerusalem (Acts 6:3). Hence the employment of this somewhat specialized verb rather than the more frequently-used terms for "appoint" suggests that its special characteristics should be understood.[4]

Because this brother had been selected by each of the churches, rather than by Paul himself, no charge of "cronyism" or undue collaboration could be sustained against Paul in the matter of these financial affairs. Even though the work of the collection ("this grace," KJV) was clearly under Paul's direction, he was taking due precaution to avoid any taint of impropriety. He wanted to make sure that a successful collection would

3. Views which suggest any Macedonians (such as Aristarchus, Sopater, Secundus, or Gaius) as candidates meet an objection at 9:4, where Paul's mention of an embarrassing situation for the Corinthians is difficult to understand if a Macedonian brother had already gone to Corinth with Titus. This objection is not insurmountable, however, for Titus' companions did not expect the collection at Corinth to be completed before their arrival, and hence 9:4 refers to an additional stage of the collection.

4. The same arguments can be employed for the only other New Testament use of this verb (Acts 14:23). See Homer A. Kent, Jr., *Jerusalem to Rome*, pp. 118-119.

promote the glory of God, and display the readiness of Paul[5] and his party to remember the needs of the poor as he had previously promised (Gal. 2:10).

VERSE 20. The apostle expected the collection to be a generous one. At the same time, he recognized that any considerable amount of funds given for charitable purposes opens the collectors to suspicion if safeguards are not provided. Anyone in the limelight as Paul was quickly learns that his prominence makes him an obvious target of critics, especially in financial matters. Once suspicions are aroused, they will color every future action. It is absolutely essential, therefore, that suitable precautions be taken. Paul was doing exactly that. By using a delegation of trustworthy men, and getting authorization from a spectrum of churches, he was avoiding any possibility of serious suspicion.

VERSE 21. By taking forethought to act in a clearly honorable way, Paul displayed true spirituality coupled with deep practical wisdom. Through the special procedures he has outlined above, he was making sure that the Lord's will would be accomplished and that people would not misunderstand his actions. Occasionally one hears a Christian leader foolishly say, "I am a servant of Christ, and I do not need to be concerned with what men think." To Paul, however, it mattered very much what people thought. If his ministry in this collection were misunderstood, the whole project could be wrecked. God's servants must give attention both to the doing of God's will and to making sure that reasonable men do not misunderstand. The thought and terminology may have been drawn from Proverbs 3:4.

c. Our brother (8:22)

VERSE 22. The third member of the delegation is merely called "our brother." That he was not Paul's physical brother is virtually certain from the complete absence of any other hint that Paul had such a brother as an associate, the fact that sending a family member on this kind of mission could arouse rather than alleviate suspicion, and that "brother" was quite

5. Although most manuscripts, including the principal uncials, read *prothumian hēmōn* ("our readiness"), a few have *prothumian humōn* ("your readiness"), and the latter has been followed by KJV. Documentary evidence, however, clearly supports the former.

commonly a Pauline designation for a fellow Christian (1:1). The expression here is similar to the one in 8:18.

This brother is likewise unnamed, but would have been readily identified when the letter reached its first readers (see discussion about 8:18). In distinction from "the brother" previously mentioned, "our brother" may have been one of Paul's associates. However, he, too, was authorized by the churches (8:23), and was characterized by diligence and a deep interest in the collection project at Corinth. This brother's interest had probably increased after Titus' report (7:6-7), and he was confident[6] that the Corinthians would vindicate his enthusiasm for them and the task. Perhaps he, too, was among the group listed in Acts 20:4.

d. Commendation of the group (8:23-24)

VERSE 23. The clauses of this verse are somewhat elliptical, and KJV has conveyed the sense well. Paul seemed to anticipate possible questions about the authorization of these delegates, and therefore gave a brief summation. Titus was Paul's well-known associate, and had already been his coworker in matters regarding Corinth, having just returned from a mission there (7:6-7). The other two "brothers" were duly authorized delegates[7] of the churches involved in the collection project. Apparently both were selected by the churches, but "our brother" (8:22) had the additional distinction of being one of Paul's associates. By their lives and ministry they had brought glory to Christ, and the present mission would bring opportunity to do so again.

VERSE 24. The Corinthians, therefore, were to display to these delegates the love about which Paul had boasted. By so doing, they would be displaying their response, as it were, to other churches which were observ-

6. The Greek text does not make it certain whether the confidence was Paul's (KJV) or belonged to "our brother" (NASB, NIV), although word order would tend toward the latter.

7. The term is *apostoloi*. These, however, are not called "apostles of Christ," as were the Twelve and Paul, but apostles of the churches, that is, ones deriving their authorization from various local congregations. A similar New Testament example is Epaphroditus (Phil. 2:25).

Fig. 10. Sidewalk at ancient Corinth, with curbing and gutter.

ing them (cf. 9:2, 3). A hearty contribution would vindicate Paul's boasting, and clearly show that love was not an absent virtue in the Corinthian church.

2. Exhortation to readiness (9:1-5)

VERSE 1. The main details about the collection were well known to the Corinthians, both from previous personal contacts with Titus and possibly Paul himself, and also from the earlier discussion in this epistle (chap. 8). Therefore, "to go on writing"[8] about it was not really necessary.

VERSE 2. What Paul was doing in this paragraph was urging the

8. The infinitive *to graphein* is present tense, emphasizing progressive action: "to continue writing."

Corinthians to bring their project to a conclusion. Their eagerness or readiness of mind had been quick to accept the challenge in the past, and presumably they had made a start toward gathering the funds. Paul had used this enthusiastic beginning to stimulate the Macedonians toward a similar response. This statement clearly indicates that Paul was presently in Macedonia. Whenever he had occasion to speak about the collection, he would boast about those of Achaia, of which Corinth was the capital. (This epistle was addressed not only to Corinth, but to the surrounding churches as well, 1:1). The Achaians' readiness of which he spoke was their willingness to accept the task, and does not contradict their possible unpreparedness (9:4), which refers to the completion of the task.

Using the Corinthians and their neighboring Christians as an example for the Macedonians had been effective. The Corinthians' zeal had stimulated most of the Macedonian Christians into accepting the challenge. They had worked harder because their Corinthian neighbors to the south had set a good example.

VERSE 3. The possibility existed, however, that both Paul and the Christians at Corinth might face embarrassment if good intentions did not lead to a successful completion. For this reason Paul was sending[9] three Christian brethren (i.e., Titus and two others, 8:16-24) to assist the Corinthians in finishing the collection. He wanted to be sure that readiness of mind was matched by achievement. Anything less would empty his boasts about them of any real effect, and could well cause a negative reaction to the whole project.

VERSE 4. When Paul would make his next visit to Corinth (which would be his third one, 12:14; 13:1), he might be accompanied by some Macedonian believers. If it should happen that they would find the Corinthians to be lacking in action as compared to Paul's boast about them, it could be acutely embarrassing to Paul, and even more so to the Corinthians themselves. Paul's confident assurance of the Corinthians' generous spirit would be seen as lacking a basis. Although Paul softened the bluntness of this remark by mentioning his embarrassment first, it should have been

9. Epistolary aorist: *epempsa*.

obvious that the real embarrassment would belong to the church at Corinth.

VERSE 5. Paul sent Titus and the other two in advance of his own visit so that the organizational aspects of the offering might be fully carried out. The real problem lay not in an unwillingness to give, but in a lack of proper organization for expediting the project. A certain disorderliness and lack of unity seem to have characterized the church at Corinth (I Cor. 14:40; 16:16).

The word "bounty" (KJV; "bountiful gift," NASB) is the term that is frequently translated "blessing" (*eulogian*). The two meanings are closely related, for a blessing conveyed to someone may also be a generous gift to him. In this case, the Corinthians' blessing on the needy at Jerusalem would take the form of a bountiful gift of money. The Corinthians had promised to provide such a blessing. It was time that they take the steps to make it a reality.

With proper preparation, Paul expected the Corinthians' gift to be generous and thus an exceptional blessing to the needy. It should not be skimpy, the sort that a covetous man, who wanted to keep as much as possible for himself, would give.

D. The Results of Generous Giving (9:6-15)

1. Increased blessing to the giver (9:6-11)

VERSE 6. Using the familiar figure of sowing and reaping (Prov. 11:24; Gal. 6:7), Paul stressed the thought that giving in this God-directed way is an investment whose returns are in proportion to what is invested. A farmer may have looked wasteful as he threw his seed on the plowed ground, but the harvest he would receive had a direct relationship to the quantity of seed that was sown. In like manner a Christian may appear foolish when he gives to others out of meager resources, but he is investing in the Lord's work, and the harvest will be commensurate with the planting.

VERSE 7. Consequently, each believer should first decide in his own heart what would be appropriate for him to give in light of what God has done for him, and then he should act. The point stressed here is that the giving should be in accord with one's inner motives. "Not grudgingly, or of necessity" (KJV) is, literally, "not out of grief or of compulsion." We should not give if we are sorry about it or feel pressured into it. This statement was not meant to discourage giving, but to make the giver examine his motives. If one gives with wrong motives, he should change his motives, not stop giving. A biblical example of giving which did not proceed from the heart but from external factors (perhaps the pressure of group opinion) is that of Ananias and Sapphira, who were not required to give, but misrepresented what was given so as to gain group approval and still retain part of the money for themselves (Acts 5:1-11).

"God loves a cheerful giver." Of course, God loves all His children, even those who do not give. The point is that giving willingly from the heart pleases Him, and this should encourage every Christian to give with cheerfulness,[10] not with misgivings or second thoughts.

VERSE 8. The cheerful giver has the promise that God will in turn make every grace abound to him. Generosity in giving by believers will never leave God indebted to us, for He always returns far more than we can ever give. The interpretation of "all grace" should not be limited to material blessings, for the term includes His spiritual gifts as well. By supplying "all" (*pasan*) grace in "everything" (*panti*) and "always" (*pantote*), the believer can have "all" sufficiency (*pasan*) so as to abound in "every" good work (*pan*). The emphasis on "all" or "every" can hardly be missed. Giving is one of God's gifts of grace, and He can produce that gift in us, just as He produces all other graces. If we do not give, we are rejecting one of God's gracious gifts to us.

VERSE 9. In a quotation of Psalm 112:9, Paul reinforced his previous statement by showing from Scripture that the righteous man, the one who fears the Lord (Ps. 112:1), will demonstrate his righteousness by righteous deeds. Using the figure of sowing, just as Paul had done in 9:6, the psalm describes the righteous man as dispensing generously to those in need, and such righteous deeds have eternal implications, for God takes notice and approves this kind of action.

10. Although the Greek word *hilaron* is the root of the English terms *hilarious* and *exhilaration,* it would be incorrect to translate the phrase as "a hilarious giver." The English connotation of frivolity or boisterous gaiety was never implicit or explicit in the Greek term.

VERSE 10. Continuing the figure of sowing, Paul wove together terminology from Isaiah 55:10 and Hosea 10:12 to remind his readers that God has supplied the generous giver with the resources out of which he gives. In the metaphor, the farmer has actually gotten his seed from God (that is, seed is no manufactured product), and the resultant crop which provides his food and also supplies more seed is likewise the act of God. In a similar way, God will provide for the believer who sows seed by generous giving. The righteous actions of believers in this matter of giving will yield great results as the lives of others are blessed.

VERSE 11. Paul was certain that God Himself would be enriching[11] the lives of the Corinthians, not just by material provisions, but with every sort of spiritual grace that would increase their generous qualities and prompt an increasing concern for the needs of others.

Consequently Paul and his associates would be God's instruments ("through us") to accomplish these purposes, and the result would be an outpouring of praise to God from everyone involved—the recipients of the gift, the generous givers, and the agents whom God had used.

2. Increased thanksgiving to the Lord (9:12-15)

VERSE 12. The thought of thanksgiving was introduced in the previous verse, but is now developed more precisely. Although the Corinthians' offering would greatly assist the economic plight of the Jerusalem Christians, it would do far more than that. It would be "overflowing in many expressions of thanks to God" (NIV). The resultant praise to God which the grateful Jerusalem Christians would offer was a spiritual matter of great value. Even the Corinthians' "service" was looked at as a specialized kind of ministration to God. The original term (*leitourgias*) often denoted either a political service to the state or priestly performance (our word *liturgy* is

11. The unusual grammatical construction of the nominative participle *ploutizomenoi* ("being enriched") can be explained in several ways. It could be governed by the subject "you" in the second clause of 9:8, and thus be parallel to *echontes* ("having"). Another possibility is to regard it as part of a periphrastic verb with the finite form *este* ("you are") or *esesthe* ("you will be") understood.

derived from this Greek term).[12] In the present instance the idea of a spiritual and religious dimension in the collection project is not difficult to see.

VERSE 13. Performance of this ministry of giving would provide a proof to the Jerusalem Christians of the genuineness of the Corinthians' confession. Perhaps there had been some doubts in Jerusalem and elsewhere, in view of the recent disorders at Corinth. Did some of the Jewish believers in Palestine suspect that the Gentile converts were not really separated from their pagan practices, and did not feel a genuine sense of unity with the body of Christ in other places? A generous act of giving would demonstrate that the Corinthians had submitted from the heart to the obligations of the gospel which they had professed (Rom. 15:27). It would also reveal the generosity that accompanied their sense of fellowship with the Jerusalem Christians and others as well. This in turn would prompt the recipients of the gift to give glory[13] to God for creating such a response to the collection project.

VERSE 14. The Corinthians' bountiful giving would cause the Jerusalem saints to reciprocate, not by a return gift of money at this time—a situation clearly impossible—but by heartfelt prayers on their behalf. As the Jerusalem Christians prayed for their Corinthian benefactors, their hearts would be knit together with them, and they would yearn for a closer association because the lavish gift ("the surpassing grace of God") which God had enabled them to give showed that they were one in spirit.

VERSE 15. The preceding verse traced the Corinthians' giving to God's grace as a cause for thanksgiving. Hence it is not surprising to find Paul's thought leaping to God's supreme gift of Christ at Calvary, for it is His redeeming grace through Christ which is the basis for all the other graces which God produces in the believer's life. Inasmuch as Paul called this gift "indescribable," any lesser identification than the one given above seems out of place.

12. R. Meyer, "Leitourgeō, Leitourgia, et al.," TDNT, IV, 215-225.

13. The participle *doxazontes* ("glorifying") is best regarded as an independent nominative. It cannot be parallel to *ploutizomenoi* (9:11, "being enriched"), inasmuch as it refers to different persons.

That Paul's encouragements to the Corinthians eventually resulted in their participation is stated in a later epistle. When Paul himself reached Corinth, he wrote to the church at Rome that Achaia had joined the project along with Macedonia (Rom. 15:26).

Questions for Discussion

1. If one's activity has a worthy Christian goal, does it matter what other people may think about that activity? Why?
2. Is it proper to make appeals for funds for various Christian enterprises? What safeguards should be observed?
3. In what ways is Christian giving like the sowing of seed?
4. Why did Paul teach that Christian giving is itself a gift from God?
5. What is God's indescribable gift? Why did Paul mention it in this context?

PAUL'S APOSTOLIC AUTHORITY

(II Corinthians 10–13)

10

Paul's Apostolic Authority

II Corinthians 10

A threat to Paul's apostolic authority may seem strange to modern readers. We view Paul from the perspective of centuries which have vindicated his ministry. But during his lifetime he paid a price that many men of God have had to pay. Jealous rivals, slanderous reports, shabby treatment, innuendo, isolation—all of these were circumstances to which Paul was no stranger. Yet he never succumbed to the pressure or gave way to total despair because he understood that his authority came from the fact that he was Christ's apostle. He was not battling for personal recognition but for the honor of his Lord whom he was proud to serve.

A definite change in tone occurs at this point in II Corinthians. So pronounced is this difference that some commentators have imagined chapters 10-13 to be a fragment from a different letter.[1] (For a discussion of this problem, see "The Unity of II Corinthians" in the introduction). However, there is no evidence that II Corinthians ever circulated in a form different from the present thirteen chapters.

In fact, it is quite possible to understand that the previous chapters of II Corinthians have laid the foundation for what is to follow by clarifying certain other issues. It has been made clear that most of the matters causing tension between the church and Paul had been resolved. Paul was

---

1. A recent example is C. K. Barrett, *The Second Epistle to the Corinthians,* pp. 243-245.

overjoyed at the return of the Corinthians' warm feelings toward him. He bore them no ill will, and was confident that they shared his loving concern. Furthermore, he had discussed the collection, and had expressed his confidence that they would not disappoint him with a poor offering (9:2).

There was still one matter, however, which needed to be addressed before he came to visit them again. Paul knew that certain divisive teachers were still present at Corinth, and were circulating falsehoods about him. They no longer reflected the prevailing attitude of the congregation, but these "false apostles" still posed a threat to the progress of the church and to the success of Paul's impending visit (11:13). Consequently, this closing section of the epistle dealt with that issue in direct and forceful terms, but it was now abundantly clear that merely certain deceitful individuals, not the whole church, were being rebuked.

IV. Paul's Apostolic Authority (10:1—13:10)

A. Paul's Defense of His Authority (10:1—11:15)

1. Paul's weapons and authority (10:1-11)

VERSE 1. With the opening words "I Paul myself," the writer turned from the "we" which had included his associates to a personal vindication of himself from the charges made against him. Anticipating one of the charges, namely, that he was "timid" (NIV) when present but "bold" when writing from a distance,[2] Paul described his usual manner of treating the Corinthians with meekness and gentleness as actually "the meekness and gentleness of Christ." It not only had been a characteristic of the Lord's ministry, but also was the source of Paul's ability to perform similarly. The actual charge against Paul apparently was that he was quite lowly and undemanding whenever he was face to face with the Corinthians, but that his letters written from the safety of distance were bold or even harsh. Perhaps there is a reference here to the severe letter which he had sent not

2. The punctuation in NIV makes this clear.

too long before (2:4, 9; 7:8-12; see Introduction, "Background"). Paul had explained his procedure: he wrote directly and forcefully so that problems could be rectified before he visited them. Thus his visits could be gentle and positive, not disciplinary (I Cor. 4:21).

VERSE 2. Paul requested the Corinthian believers to carry out fully their resolve (7:6-16) to rectify the problems in their congregation before he arrived. He did not wish to be forced into a situation where he had to use the boldness of his apostolic authority to rebuke the church.

Nevertheless Paul was under no illusions about whether some individuals would need an apostolic rebuke. The church as a whole may have mellowed in its attitude toward Paul, but there were still some detractors whom he was prepared to confront.

These opponents regarded both him and his associates[3] as if they "walked according to the flesh." It is not indicated whether these individuals ever stated this, but the things they did say reflected their estimation of Paul. The way they treated the apostolic party and the things they said about the apostolic group made it clear these opponents thought the missionaries' conduct was not led by the Holy Spirit, but proceeded from mere human motivation and ingenuity. The reference to "the flesh" should not cause us to suppose accusations of immorality, for which there could hardly have been any basis, but charges of assuming unwarranted authority, dictatorial methods, and perhaps inconsistency and pride.

VERSE 3. Paul explained that he and the others did walk "in the flesh," but he made a distinction here between "in the flesh" (*en sarki*) and "according to the flesh" (*kata sarka*). The former is a reference to the possession of a human body with all its present frailties. This use of the phrase occurs in Galatians 2:20 ("the life which I now live in the flesh") and Philippians 1:22 ("if I am to live on in the flesh"). It was a reminder to his readers that his ministry did not protect him from human ailments, suffering, and mistreatment.

Nevertheless, true servants of God do not carry out their ministries

3. Here the plural is used, for these detractors apparently had a low view of Paul's entire missionary party. The singular pronouns are resumed later in the discussion.

"according to the flesh." That is, they do not let mere human factors provide the norms nor the power for their ministries. Recognizing that Christian ministry is a warfare against a foe who is not earthly and human, the perceptive servant of Christ will carry out his campaign with all the seriousness which it deserves. He will identify the enemy correctly, he will recognize the true issues involved, and he will do battle, equipped with the appropriate weapons.

VERSE 4. The only weapons which are ultimately effective for this kind of warfare are not "of the flesh." Human eloquence, manmade schemes, personal magnetism, psychological manipulation, crowd dynamics, and showmanship may achieve temporary results, but ultimately they are no match for the opposing spiritual forces. In a later epistle, Paul explained that "we wrestle not against flesh and blood, but . . . against spiritual wickedness in high places" (Eph. 6:12, KJV).

Paul relied on spiritual resources that were "divinely powerful"[4] for the tearing down of fortresses. His weapons were not just defensive to ward off attacks from others, but had positive effects in destroying certain aspects of the enemy's power. Paul's weapons were divinely energized and thus were more than a match for any earthly foe as well as for any satanic opposition.

VERSE 5. What enemy fortresses did Paul have in mind? The following phrases explain his metaphor. "Destroying speculations" refers to the human reasonings and philosophies which are opposed to God. The true servants of God are not simply preaching one more human religion. They are the Spirit-empowered agents of God, and are given the spiritual weaponry whereby even the most intellectual of human philosophies can be unmasked.

"Every lofty thing raised up" is a further explanation of the metaphor. In this spiritual warfare which the true apostles of Christ waged, the particular

4. The dative *tōi theōi* in the phrase *dunata tōi theōi* (literally, "powerful to God") has been variously understood. 1) It can express instrument or means, hence "mighty through God" (KJV). 2) It can be a dative of advantage: "mighty for God." 3) It can be a superlative, based on a Hebraism (as in Acts 7:20), and similar to modern Greek which compounds word with *theō-* (see Barrett, *Second Epistle,* p. 251). 4) It can be a dative of respect: "with respect to God," "before God" (ASV). The exposition given above has adopted a combination of 1 and 3.

objects of attack were the fortresses of human reasoning. These are now explained as those human philosophies regarding God and His works which are contrary to what God Himself has revealed. Such philosophies are "against the knowledge of God," for they place their own explanations above God's revelation. In a previous letter to the Corinthians, Paul had labeled the wisdom of the world as "foolish," and had shown that God's saving message is indeed the only truth which contains the power and wisdom to redeem lost men (I Cor. 1:18-31).

Through the use of the spiritual weapons that Christ supplied, Paul and his assistants not only attacked the opposing fortresses of religious error, but also engaged in "taking every thought captive to the obedience of Christ." This statement does not describe Paul's commitment of his own thought processes to Christ, but refers to overcoming and capturing the human wisdom promoted by enemies of the gospel. Paul had been ministering in such a way that many of his hearers had come out of darkness into light; they had given up the wisdom of this world, and had become submissive to the lordship of Christ in thought as well as deed.

VERSE 6. The readers must not suppose, therefore, that Paul was unequipped to deal with difficult matters. He had the spiritual weapons from Christ his Lord. In the exercise of his apostolic office, he and his party would not hesitate to discriminate true Christian conduct from that which was disobedient to the Word of God. The readers could expect this to be accomplished on his next visit to Corinth.

"Whenever your obedience is complete" is best understood as implying Paul's expectation that the church as a whole would comply with his appeal. The believers had already made a good start (7:9, 11, 13). He had confidence that they would follow through so that when he arrived, no unpleasantness would mar the joy of their reunion. Nevertheless he was prepared to deal firmly with the few who were still recalcitrant, but only after every reasonable attempt at solution had been exhausted.

VERSE 7. The verb "look" (*blepete*) can be understood in at least three ways in this verse. It can be understood as an imperative: "Look at the things in front of you" (paraphrase of RSV). It can be an indicative with a declarative sense: "You are looking at outward appearances" (paraphrase of

NASB, NIV). Here "the things before your face" (*ta kata prosōpon*) are regarded as unsatisfactory. Or the verb can be an indicative with an interrogative sense: "Are you looking at outward appearances?" (paraphrase of KJV). All three make good sense in this passage, and are equally possible from the grammar. One's choice, therefore, is largely based on personal preference.

To this writer there seems to be slightly more reason to treat the statement as a command: "Look at the evidence." The latter part of the verse challenges the reader to consider the case of Paul as compared to the conclusions he had drawn about himself. Was there someone who insisted that he was superior to Paul in authority, that he was Christ's in a special way? Paul challenged such people to consider the facts. Paul possessed the very criteria that these people would use to argue that they were Christ's. If this reference was to those interlopers who would remain disobedient and would require Paul's discipline when he came, then he was simply taking them at their own estimate of themselves for the sake of argument. On the other hand, he might have referred to some of the true Christians at Corinth who were generally supportive but had been infected with some doubts as to Paul's authority. Perhaps such had once been members of the "Christ party" (I Cor. 1:12), which seems no longer to have been an issue by the time II Corinthians was written (at least, there is no mention of it). Paul urged these people who were so certain that they were Christians to acknowledge the same of Paul and his associates, for it was they who had brought the Christian faith to Corinth.

VERSE 8. Recognizing that he might be regarded as emphasizing unduly the authority which he had from Christ (and which he exercised with the help of his associates), Paul mentioned two significant factors. The first was that this authority was for the Corinthians' good, not their harm (these same words are repeated in 13:10). He was protecting the saints, not tearing them down. Thus any apparent harshness would be ultimately beneficial. The second factor to be recognized was that Paul was confident about his position. He knew that nothing would be uncovered which would show he had overstepped his authority. Thus he had no reason to fear the possibility of being put to shame.

Fig. 11. Acrocorinth, the hill outside Corinth on which the Temple of Aphrodite was located.

VERSE 9. If the readers would recognize the constructive nature of Paul's authority as explained in 10:8, they would know that he was not trying merely to terrify them by his letters. His purpose was to build them up, and terrifying per se would not accomplish this end.

VERSE 10. Unfortunately it was being reported that there was a striking difference between Paul's letters and his presence. "They say" (KJV, NASB) or "some say" (NIV) should be "he says," inasmuch as the verb is singular.[5] This suggests that a particular opponent may be in Paul's mind. Paul's letters were reported as "weighty and strong," powerful enough to frighten readers by their sternness. This was doubtless a reference to the lost letter (I Cor. 5:9), I Corinthians, and the severe letter (II Cor. 2:3-4), whose cumulative effect certainly must have been powerful.

On the other hand, it was said that "in person he is unimpressive and his speaking amounts to nothing" (NIV). Often this is explained as a reference to Paul's physical appearance, and the early account in the *Acts of Paul and Thekla* is cited.[6] However, to call Paul "unimpressive" in the sense of "weak" (*asthenēs*) hardly fits the New Testament account of him as a vigorous traveler, surviving all sorts of hardships and mistreatment. To regard his speaking ability as mediocre is difficult to understand in the light of the Lystrans who called him Hermes because of his speaking (Acts 14:12).

It is better to view the statement as a derogatory reaction of an opponent who was referring not so much to Paul's physical appearance as to the effect of his presence at Corinth. Perhaps this opponent was thinking of the "painful visit" when Paul's presence accomplished little. He had come without any trappings of power, nor did he have the eloquence of an Apollos. Plummer reminds us that at Troas he did not keep Eutychus awake (Acts 20:9).[7] The implication was that Paul could be disregarded, for he was not actually as authoritative as his letters might lead one to believe.

VERSE 11. "Such a person" refers to the individual quoted in verse 10, but enlarges the reference to include all who were like him. In response to the charge that Paul's manner did not match his actions, the apostle said that such a report was false. Any who kept spreading it should be warned

5. The singular reading *phēsin* is supported by the major Greek manuscripts. The plural *phasin*, however, is found in B and the Latin and Syriac versions.

6. In this apocryphal work, Paul is described as "a man little of stature, thin-haired upon the head, crooked in the legs, of good state of body, with eyebrows joining, and nose somewhat hooked, full of grace: for sometimes he appeared like a man, and sometimes he had the face of an angel." Montague Rhodes James, *The Apocryphal New Testament*, p. 273.

7. Alfred Plummer, *Corinthians Two*, p. 283.

that Paul and his associates spoke with one voice, whether present or absent. A grave mistake would be made if anyone confused graciousness with timidity, and assumed that Paul was weak and vacillating. His imminent visit (12:14) would make his consistency very evident.

2. Paul's field of service (10:12-18)

VERSE 12. In this paragraph Paul spoke of the sphere of ministry which had been given to him, and which he endeavored to occupy fully but not to exceed. Some of his opponents, however, showed no sensitivity to this sort of divine appointment.

The argument began with a bit of irony. Was Paul really timid, and thus hypocritical, as his detractors alleged? He had denied this in the portion of the letter immediately preceding, but he stated wryly that there was one matter about which he had no boldness. He and his associates did not have the daring to classify or compare themselves with some of the boasted accomplishments of the self-accredited teachers at Corinth. These teachers had promoted themselves and their teaching as superior to Paul's. They had created their own norms, and thus were measuring themselves by themselves and comparing themselves with themselves. By so doing, they naturally saw to it that they excelled, and at the same time were able to denigrate Paul. He quite understandably said that he didn't expect to measure up to such rigged standards. Nor would he wish to be grouped with such teachers. Persons who measure themselves by their own yard-sticks "are not wise" (KJV), said Paul, for they have rejected all objectivity and have no standard but themselves.

VERSE 13. Paul and his associates would not boast on the basis of any nonauthentic measurement. The measure Paul used was the one which God Himself had measured out for him. He explained that God had granted him an allotment of ministry which reached as far as the Corinthians. He referred to his apostleship, which involved bringing the gospel to a lost world with particular emphasis on the Gentile world (Gal. 2:8). Within this sphere of ministry, which had been clearly recognized earlier by the leaders of the church at Jerusalem (Gal. 2:9), Paul had brought the gospel to Corinth and had become the spiritual father of their church (I Cor. 4:15).

Could the troublemakers at Corinth point to any such divine authorization? They had no such God-given sphere directly allotted to them.

VERSE 14. "For we are not overextending ourselves, as if we did not reach to you." Paul indicated that his previous statements were not an exaggeration of his God-given field of service. If he had not reached Corinth on his missionary travels, perhaps the troublesome teachers might have had an excuse to keep him out. But the fact was, he *had* come to Corinth. In truth, he and his missionary party "were the first[8] to come even as far as you." Thus he had established the Corinthian church on virgin territory. His opponents were interlopers, poaching on his labors and undercutting his influence among his own spiritual children.

VERSE 15. This verse picks up the thought of verse 13. Paul would not boast "beyond our limits" (NIV) by implying that other men's accomplishments were his own. This was what false apostles regularly did when they moved into established churches and tried to take them over. Such boasting was not based on the measured limits (*ametra*) which God had assigned as the territory for ministry. Paul, however, regarded his assignment as taking the gospel to new territory where no other Christian workers had gone.

In contrast to unwarranted boasting, which seems to have characterized some people at Corinth, Paul had hopes that the Corinthian church would grow in spiritual understanding and appreciation of his ministry. This, however, was not merely a desire to be vindicated and more warmly praised, but to have his evangelistic labors greatly increased. The next verse explains the nature of this enlargement of his ministry.

VERSE 16. Paul's goal was to preach the gospel "in the regions beyond you" (KJV). From other references it may be concluded that Rome and Spain may have been in mind as he wrote (Acts 19:21; Rom. 15:24). However, he had no desire to move in on another man's appointed sphere of

---

8. The basic meaning of the verb *phthanō* is "to come first." In the New Testament it has this use in I Thessalonians 4:15. Other New Testament occurrences have the meaning "to arrive at" or "to reach." In II Corinthians 10:14 either sense is possible, but the former seems especially appropriate to the context, where Paul is arguing for his prior claim to the allegiance of his readers.

ministry, as these disrupting teachers at Corinth had done. He did not regard his God-given ministry as that of building on what others had previously "made ready" (KJV). His sphere of service was pioneer missionary work. Not everyone is called to this particular ministry, and it is certainly not wrong to build on another's labors. Paul himself had said, "I planted, Apollos watered" (I Cor. 3:6). What was wrong at Corinth was that certain "waterers" were taking credit for the planting, and were discrediting the planter. Paul was so convinced that he was to do pioneering work that he even regarded his proposed visit to the already-established church at Rome to be merely a stopover on his way to Spain (Rom. 15:24).

VERSE 17. Citing somewhat freely Jeremiah 9:23-24 (also quoted in I Cor. 1:31), Paul affirmed that the only legitimate boasting for any Christian must be in the Lord, who deserves the credit. The passage in Jeremiah warns against the human tendency to glory in wisdom, strength, and riches, and commands men rather to glory in the knowledge of the sovereign God who performs loving-kindness, judgment, and righteousness on the earth. On that occasion when Paul said that one may plant and another may water, he also said that God causes the growth (I Cor. 3:6-7).

VERSE 18. The real approval of one's service for God is not based on self-commendation, but on the Lord's commendation. Paul always insisted that whatever successes he had were the results of God's working through him. What might appear at times to be human boasting by Paul are seen to be boasting in the Lord on closer examination.

Several examples demonstrate this. When Paul and Barnabas returned to Antioch from their first missionary journey, they reported "all things that God had done with them and how He had opened a door of faith to the Gentiles" (Acts 14:27). A few months after writing II Corinthians Paul wrote to the Romans while he was visiting in Corinth. In that letter he explained that he was "boasting in things pertaining to God" (Rom. 15:17), but in doing so he would "not presume to speak of anything except what Christ has accomplished through me" (Rom. 15:18).

How does the Lord commend His workers? Of course, at the judgment seat of Christ this will ultimately be done (5:10). However, there is a more immediate commendation that Paul doubtless had in mind. He had explained to the Corinthians what his relations to them had been (10:14). Rather than praise himself or rely on letters of recommendation from others (3:1), he would depend on the Lord's operation on the consciences of the Corinthians. This would enable them to see in the very existence of themselves as a church the divine approval of Paul's ministry.

Questions for Discussion

1. What is the difference between "being in the flesh" and "walking according to the flesh"?
2. In what sense did Paul take every thought captive to Christ?
3. What were some of the reasons why Paul's letters were sometimes stern?
4. What did Paul consider his sphere of service to be?
5. In the light of Paul's statements, what do you think his opponents were saying about him?
6. Why do you think God often allows His greatest servants to face so much opposition?
7. What do you find most effective about Paul's handling of the problems discussed in this chapter?

11

Paul's Personal Concern
II Corinthians 11:1-15

The intelligent exercise of authority is no easy task. Power can be attractive for its own sake. Directing the lives of others can make one forget the God-given purpose of authority, which is to provide organization and leadership for the benefit of everyone. When authority is used chiefly for personal gain, the reasons for which authority has been granted have been violated.

Consequently the apostle Paul made it clear to his readers at Corinth that he had a personal concern for them. It was because he cared so deeply for them that he was willing to use some of the more unpleasant aspects of authority to protect them from false teachers and wrong teaching. Paul clearly understood the proper balance between authority and personal concern. Concern alone could result in mere sentimentality and absence of decisive action. Authority alone could be harsh and unfeeling. When apostolic authority was tempered with genuine concern for individuals, the spiritual development of the Corinthians' lives had every reason for success.

Leaders who intend to follow biblical principles would do well to study carefully the apostle's policy. Christian society has suffered much when leaders have exercised authority without demonstrating a concern for others. Paul made no such mistake.

3. Paul's jealousy for the Corinthians (11:1-6)

VERSE 1. Paul was about to compare himself with some other men (11:6). At the same time he was aware that he had just declared that self-commendation has little value (10:17-18). Of course, there was a great difference between promoting oneself for personal gain or for subversive purposes as opposed to claiming one's legitimate authority. Because self-appointed religious hucksters were perverting the message of the gospel which Christ had authorized him to proclaim, Paul felt compelled to speak as he did. His claim of authority was really his defense of the authorization for his message.

"A little of my foolishness" (NIV) was a self-deprecating statement that revealed Paul's embarrassment in being driven to such measures. From one standpoint he doubtless felt foolish in talking about his apostolic authority, for it should have been self-evident in the light of his remarkable career. On the other hand, he did not really regard it as foolish but necessary, and that was why he proceeded to discuss the matter.

After this somewhat apologetic request for the Corinthians to bear with him in his rehearsing of his personal qualifications, Paul quickly added, "But indeed you are bearing with me."[1] By this gracious statement he acknowledged their previous instances of compliance and his confidence that they would listen to him this time also.

VERSE 2. In Paul's relationship with the Corinthian believers, he had fathered them in the faith. Now he adopted the figure of betrothal and pictured himself as the father of the bride. At their conversion these believers had collectively become the betrothed bride of Christ. In the marriage custom of that day, the legal arrangements and transactions took place at the betrothal. At a later time when the wedding occurred, the primary activity involved taking the bride to the groom's home, and the celebration feast. During the interval, there was still opportunity for unfaithfulness to occur, and every upright father felt obligated to protect

1. The verb *anechesthe* can be either indicative (as rendered by NASB, NIV) or imperative (KJV, "and indeed bear with me"). The use of the strong adversative "but" (*alla*) makes the former more likely, in the opinion of this writer.

his virgin daughter until the marriage was consummated. So Paul felt obligated to protect the purity of the Corinthian church until Christ should come. He wished to make sure that the church Christ would find at His coming was a pure one, not adulterated with falsity of doctrine or of life.

Although the spiritual concern which Paul felt is commonly translated as "a godly jealousy," it could just as well be rendered as "God's jealousy" or "the jealousy of God" (*theou zēlōi*). It was no mere human jealousy over losing his followers to a rival. Rather, he was moved by God's point of view which regarded instability toward the gospel as spiritual adultery (James 4:4).

VERSE 3. What made Paul fearful was his concern over the deceitfulness of some teachers who had been most persuasive as they had contacted the Corinthians. This deceitfulness reminded him of the craftiness of the serpent in the deception of Eve in the Garden of Eden. Just as the serpent deceived Eve by convincing her that God's Word was not reliable (Gen. 3:4-5),[2] so the Corinthians were running the risk of similar deception as long as they tolerated the presence of improper teachers. If the Corinthians listened to false teachers instead of to the true apostles of Christ, they stood in great danger of having their minds led astray from the simplicity and the purity which they owed to Christ. As a loving but concerned spiritual father, Paul wanted no impurity to mar the nuptial joy when Christ would come to claim His bride. Such a jealousy is always in order.

VERSE 4. Paul focused his fears more precisely on a situation which was probably occurring in Corinth. "If one comes and preaches another Jesus" described a false teacher who was not sent or authorized by anyone. This person arrived on his own. He did not preach another Christ, that is, a different person with messianic claims. What was proclaimed was such an alteration in the true nature and work of Jesus of Nazareth that for all

2. The illustration should not be pressed to make Eve's sin a sexual one with the serpent, as some Jewish commentators did. The analogy would not be accurate for Eve was a married woman, not a betrothed virgin. Paul emphasized the concept of the mind or thoughts being led astray, not that of morals being corrupted. The seduction had to do not with sex but with doctrine.

practical purposes He became "another Jesus." Perhaps His deity was denied, or the true significance of His crucifixion.

"Or you receive a different spirit which you have not received [from us]." Paul's preaching had resulted in regeneration and the indwelling of the Holy Spirit. False teaching, however, is the product of a different sort of spirit (I John 4:1). It may be that the reference to "spirit" connotes various products which the Holy Spirit produces—liberty (3:17), power (II Tim. 1:7), peace and joy (Rom. 14:17), in contrast to a "spirit of bondage" (Rom. 8:15).[3]

A "different gospel" denotes any so-called good news which fails to proclaim the true Christ and His saving work (Gal. 1:6-7). The conversion of the Corinthians had been brought about when they accepted the true gospel through the preaching of Paul. Why should they now pay attention to a different sort of message?

With some irony[4] Paul concluded, "You bear this beautifully." It was strange that the Corinthians should show such toleration for a perverted message, when so recently they had been highly critical of Paul.

VERSE 5. That Paul still smarted from some of the slights and accusations he had experienced from the Corinthians may be concluded from his next statement. He was defending himself from the insinuations that had been made about him. Thus he asserted that in no respect had he been inferior to "super-apostles" (NIV).

To whom was Paul referring as "super-apostles"? One view regards them as the Twelve, or perhaps Peter, James, and John (Gal. 2:9). Inasmuch as Paul was not averse to comparing himself to them and claiming equal apostolic authority, the reference here is interpreted in that light (as is also 12:11). This verse also has been used by Protestants to argue against the supremacy of Peter, and by various scholars as an indication of the existence of Petrine and Pauline factions in the early church. None of these conclusions is warranted, however. If some or all of the Twelve are alluded

3. Philip E. Hughes, *Commentary on the Second Epistle to the Corinthians,* pp. 377-378.
4. This feature is not conveyed clearly by the KJV, although it is almost certainly the sense intended.

to, it is likely that Paul was not being sarcastic toward them directly, but was merely alluding to the exaggerated way in which either the false teachers or the Corinthians themselves had been referring to them in disparagement of Paul.

The other possibility explains the "super-apostles" as an ironic reference to the same intruders who are called "false apostles" in 11:13. They had come to Corinth making great claims for themselves. Unfortunately, they had no authorization from Christ. On the whole, this identification seems preferable to this writer, for it is doubtful that Paul would have been criticized as a trained speaker in comparison to some spellbinding charlatan.

VERSE 6. Another criticism of Paul by his detractors was apparently his lack of training in professional rhetoric. He was willing to acknowledge that he was "one untrained in speech" (*idiōtēs tōi logōi*), but this need not imply that he was an ineffective speaker. All our evidences from the Book of Acts disprove such an inference. The term "untrained one" (*idiōtēs*) denoted a private individual as distinct from an official, or a layman as compared to an expert.[5] Hence Paul did not claim the artificial, stylized elegance of professional rhetoricians. The importance lay in the content of what was preached, not its style and trappings. In every way and in all respects Paul had manifested this knowledge[6] of God's truth to the Corinthians when he ministered the word of God to them. Surely he ought to be evaluated on the basis of essentials, not superficial matters.

4. Paul's preaching policy (11:7-11)

VERSE 7. Paul devoted a whole paragraph to answer another criticism—that his taking no pay from the church was a sin. Were his detractors saying that this was an admission that Paul was not really a qualified teacher?

Of course, Paul himself argued elsewhere that those who ministered the

5. Heinrich Schlier, "Idiōtēs," TDNT, III, 215-217.

6. The KJV adopts the passive participle variant "having been made manifest," thus referring to Paul as having been vindicated by what he preached. The active participle, however, has older manuscript support, but one must supply an object: thus, "having manifested [it, this knowledge]."

gospel had a right to expect support from those who benefited from that ministry (I Cor. 9:3-15). At Corinth, however, Paul had supported himself by tentmaking (Acts 18:3). He had humbled himself by doing manual labor during the week, thus restricting his preaching efforts for a time to the synagogue services. His sole purpose was to bring the gospel to the Corinthians without any burden whatever on them. They were elevated to the position of recipients while Paul was laboring to make it possible. By responding to the gospel, they were exalted to the status of sons of God. For anyone to suggest that Paul's humble action was sin shows how mean and ridiculous his detractors were.

VERSE 8. It must be remembered that Paul was not here accusing the Corinthians of treating him meagerly. Rather, he was responding to the accusation that his refusal to accept pay from the Corinthians was an indication that he was inferior to genuine apostles. Paul's answer should have established two facts with his readers. First, he had not refused to accept income from all churches; he had not accepted money from the Corinthians. Second, his refusal to be a financial burden to the Corinthians should have been regarded as an act of love, not a cause for criticism.

The figure of robbing other churches is, of course, hyperbole. It was robbery only in the sense that the churches who gave to Paul's support were not presently receiving the benefits and hence had no direct obligation to give.

Apparently it was Paul's regular policy to support himself and to rely on supplementary gifts from other churches whenever he was attempting to establish a new church (I Cor. 9:18). He did not wish prospective believers to conclude that they were being financially exploited. Thus Paul supported himself at Thessalonica (I Thess. 2:9; II Thess. 3:8-9) and Ephesus (Acts 20:34), as well as at Corinth.

VERSE 9. The apostle reminded his readers that during his presence with them at the founding of their church, he did not allow his financial needs to become a burden to his Corinthian friends. He had been supporting himself by tentmaking (Acts 18:3). However, this apparently was not sufficient to meet all of his needs. Yet even this stress did not cause Paul to turn to the Corinthians for support. Instead, his need was met by the arrival

Fig. 12. Columns of Temple of Apollo at Corinth. In distance, the Acrocorinth, site of the Temple of Aphrodite.

of "the brethren" who came from Macedonia. This doubtless referred to Silas and Timothy, who joined Paul at Corinth (Acts 18:5), presumably bringing a gift from the church at Philippi, which is in Macedonia (Phil. 4:15).[7] This

7. The gift mentioned in Philippians 4:15 was sent after Paul left Macedonia; hence it must be distinguished from the several gifts sent to him at Thessalonica (Phil. 4:16). Presumably it was the one sent to Paul at Corinth.

enabled Paul to spend less time at his manual labor and to concentrate his energies on preaching (Acts 18:5).

Not only in financial affairs, but "in everything" Paul had kept himself from being burdensome to the Corinthians. This had been his policy in the past and would continue to characterize his procedure with them. It was not due to lack of apostolic authority or inappropriateness, but was his own choice. Paul's point was that he had not become a burden to them, even when he might have been.

VERSE 10. With the words "the truth of Christ is in me," Paul insisted that his explanation was true and he spoke as a faithful emissary of Christ Himself. Paul had found a sense of personal satisfaction in being able to preach among the Corinthians without imposing any monetary obligations on them. It was not something to be ashamed of; certainly it was not a demeaning practice. Consequently, he felt free for "boasting" about it because it brought no credit to him, but to his Lord. Christ had supplied every need—partly by providing manual employment in Corinth, and the rest by the generous gifts of other churches. Paul did not intend to let the misinterpretation which had been placed on this policy prevent him from continuing it. It had been his general practice everywhere (I Cor. 9:18), even though he had the right to expect proper remuneration if he chose to accept it (I Cor. 9:14-15). The province of Achaia, of which Corinth was the capital, had doubtless heard already of Paul's practice, and perhaps had learned of the false charges also. At least one other church, the one at Cenchrea, had been established in Achaia by this time (Rom. 16:1), and there may have been others (II Cor. 1:1).

VERSE 11. For what possible reason could Paul have refused to take remuneration from the Corinthians other than the wholesome one he had just explained? It made no sense to suppose that his action sprang from lack of love. What he had done proved just the opposite. Only if one were predisposed to be critical of Paul for other reasons could his policy regarding money be twisted to be used against him. Paul knew his own heart, and he knew that God also understood his motives even if some men did not. The truth was that Paul had endured the rigors of extensive travel, long hours at manual labor, mistreatment from the enemies of the gospel, and shabby treatment from some Christians at Corinth to bring the message of salvation to these people and nurture them in the faith. And all of this at no charge to the Corinthians! If that is not love, what is?

5. Paul's opponents (11:12-15)

VERSE 12. Paul's policy as outlined above was adopted in order to counteract the efforts of certain opponents whom he later described as "false apostles." He would continue his policy of preaching without taking pay from the church directly involved. He wished to leave no opportunity for his opponents to gain an advantage or twist the circumstances and use them against him. He knew that the false apostles were accepting payment for their teaching, and were even using this fact as an argument that they must be superior to Paul inasmuch as genuine apostles had the right to be paid (I Cor. 9:1-14). At the same time they must have been aware that Paul's serving without remuneration had heightened the contrast between him and themselves. Any suspicion of mercenary motives would have fallen on these "false apostles," not on Paul.

The last clause of verse 12 ("that wherein they glory," KJV) should be understood as dependent on the words immediately preceding (as in NASB, NIV), rather than as parallel to the preceding clause and dependent on "I will do" (as in KJV). Paul meant that those who were glorying in their self-appointed status as "apostles" at Corinth were desirous of removing any distinction between Paul and themselves. Hence if they could somehow cause him to accept pay, he would be on the same basis as they, and the undeniable altruistic advantage which Paul had would be removed. No longer would they need to concoct some not-too-convincing explanation to disparage Paul's generous ministry at Corinth.

VERSE 13. Such persons were really "false apostles." Their falsity was in two respects: they masqueraded as apostles whom Christ had appointed, even though they had no such calling; and the message they conveyed was contrary to God's revealed truth. In their arrogance they assumed authority they did not really possess, and opposed genuine apostles such as Paul. Whether or not they ever referred to themselves in this way may be questioned, but Paul caricatured their manner and claims by the ironic term "super-apostles" (11:5, NIV).

These teachers were "deceitful workers," for their credentials were a sham, and their efforts were threatening to capture the unwary. Their understanding of Christian truth was defective, but their claims for themselves tended to conceal the inadequacies of their teaching.

VERSE 14. Such tactics on the part of false teachers should not surprise us, for they are merely following the example of Satan, their spiritual father (John 8:44). Satan transforms himself into an angel of light, and Paul's opponents were doing the same. This particular description of Satan is not found elsewhere in Scripture, but the concept is not unknown. Notions of a disgusting creature with horns, tail, and a pitchfork come from legend and allegory, not the Bible. Even the serpent whom Satan used in tempting Eve was not the crawling creature we know today (Gen. 3:1, 14). Satan was one of the angelic "sons of God" (Job 1:6; 2:1) who had direct access to God's presence.

The description of Satan in this passage is primarily of moral rather than physical characteristics. The point is that Satan influences people, not primarily by repulsive suggestions but by ideas which seem attractive on the surface. Yet his true nature is darkness, not light (Eph. 6:12).

VERSE 15. Satan carries on his works through his servants (KJV, "ministers") who derive their motivation and their methods from him. They assume the guise of promoters of righteousness, but such righteousness is a masquerade, not their true nature. The "righteousness" they promote is a self-righteousness, a righteousness of works, and this is the opposite of the message Christ brought and the true apostles proclaimed.

Paul had no hesitancy in charging these opponents with the spiritual crimes they were committing. They were proclaiming a righteousness which was not God's righteousness. They were false apostles masquerading as Christ's appointees. They were exhibiting the character and practice of Satan, the supreme deceiver. And they faced the prospect of certain judgment. When God would ultimately deal with them, it would be in absolute justice and in accordance with the true nature of their deeds, not with what they pretended to be.

Questions for Discussion

1. Why do you suppose God allowed Paul to have so many opponents? What conclusions do you draw from this fact for your life?
2. What was Paul's policy regarding being paid for preaching? Be sure you utilize all the pertinent biblical data in your answer.
3. Who were the "super-apostles" mentioned in 11:5?
4. Were the "super-apostles" the same as or different from the false apostles referred to in 11:13? What are the reasons for your decision?
5. In what sense does Satan disguise himself as an angel of light today?

12

"Boasting as a Fool"

II Corinthians 11:16—12:13

Talking about one's own accomplishments can be an awkward experience. It can easily be misunderstood as bragging. Even testimonies in which one is presumably recounting how God has enabled him to perform some remarkable action may leave the impression that a degree of self-glorification is involved. Such references can be most embarrassing to anyone who is sensitive to the possibilities of being considered egotistical. Public speakers, therefore, often apologize for making personal references. Under normal circumstances personal references should be avoided.

There are times, however, when personal explanations are necessary. In order to prevent distorted statements, unfounded gossip, or outright slander, or to protect the welfare or reputation of others, it may be one's duty to set the record straight, even when one must risk feelings of awkwardness. Surely it is essential to defend the truth and prevent the twisting of facts when the Lord's work is involved.

In Paul's case a crucial issue was at stake. Some people had raised questions about the apostleship which he exercised. The implications of this issue went very deep. Either Paul was an apostle commissioned by Jesus Christ or he was not. If he was, then his authority and teaching must be heeded at all costs. If he were not, then he was a "false apostle" whose entire ministry was suspect. The value of Paul's preaching and teaching rested squarely on the truth involved in this question.

As Paul wrote these words, the church as a whole at Corinth had rallied behind him and was responsive to his ministry (7:7-11). Because a few intruders at Corinth (whom he called "false apostles" in 11:13) were still trying to undermine his ministry, he had to discuss these matters further. At the same time it must not be forgotten that this issue is not one of historical interest only. Our Christian faith today likewise depends on the validity of the apostle's testimony. The reader will do well to study carefully Paul's explanation, and let it strengthen his confidence in the apostleship of Paul.

B. Paul's "Boasting as a Fool" (11:16—12:13)

1. Paul's reluctance explained (11:16-21a)

VERSE 16. "Again I say" is probably a reference to 11:1, where Paul also acknowledged a certain feeling of foolishness in this sort of discussion. He appealed to his readers not to regard him as a fool when he stooped to set forth these claims about himself. However, even if they would not grant this request, then he asked them to tolerate him just as they would indulge a fool for a time. He was so desirous that his readers understand his explanation that he would grasp any opportunity, even if it were not on the most favorable terms. He must defend his apostleship against the insinuations or false claims of others because the authority of Christ was at stake. Thus he asked the Corinthians to hear him out, although it might seem that his boasting about "a little something" (*mikron ti*) might appear to them as foolishness.

VERSE 17. Such speaking as Paul was about to pursue was not what he preferred, nor was it characteristic[1] of the Lord in His actions on earth. Paul readily admitted that his present tactic was not following the example of Jesus. Rather, he was attempting to "answer a fool according to his folly" (Prov. 26:5, NIV). He was not denying the inspiration and authority of his words; he was merely stating that he was forced to utilize a legitimate

1. The Greek preposition *kata* suggests a standard of measurement; hence the phrase *kata kurion* probably means "in accordance with the Lord," or "as the Lord would" (NIV).

Fig. 13. South entrance to Corinth Canal at Isthmia.

method other than the example of Christ, although it was somewhat distasteful to do so. Paul was about to recite confidently his own credentials, but it embarrassed him, and made him feel like a fool for doing so.

VERSE 18. Because "many" were engaging in promoting their ministries by publicizing their personal credentials, Paul felt compelled to do the same to vindicate the commission he had from Christ. How numerous were the "many" at Corinth is not revealed, although the number must have been large enough to threaten the welfare of the church. These opponents are also referred to as "the many" in 2:17. Their boasting was not prompted by their regenerated nature but by their natural selves ("the flesh"). Although Paul, too, was going to do some boasting, he did not intend to join the others in sinful boasting. He had made his motives clear. Therefore, he did not say that what he would do was according to the flesh. "Also" links him with the boasting, but not with "flesh."

VERSE 19. There is surely some irony in this statement. Even though the apostle felt awkward in this "boasting as a fool," he reminded the Corinthians that their sophistication ("being so wise") had been allowing them to put up with a lot of fools lately. In fact they had even done so "gladly." It should be no great thing, therefore, for them to listen to him, since they had been so tolerant of the false apostles.

VERSE 20. What the Corinthians had tolerated from the imposters was incredible. Five examples are mentioned. They had allowed themselves to be enslaved, perhaps to the imposition of the Mosaic requirements. This same problem had occurred among the Galatian churches (Gal. 4:1-11; 5:1). They had suffered the plundering efforts of the false apostles to "devour" them, a probable reference to the financial exploitation which had occurred among them, in sharp contrast to Paul's practice. Furthermore, the Corinthians had been caught (literally, "taken") by the duplicity of those teachers, and had been for a time captivated by faulty doctrine and slanderous statements about Paul. They had endured the self-exaltation of the intruders as though these teachers were true apostles.

The Corinthians had even tolerated the insult of being slapped in the face by those false apostles. This could refer to insulting language which the church had endured from those arrogant pretenders. However, it was not unknown for religious authorities to enforce their wishes by such violent measures. Paul would experience something similar at the orders of the high priest Ananias (Acts 23:2). To suppose that the Corinthians would have actually accepted such treatment and still have blindly followed those leaders would be difficult to believe if experience had not taught us that religious dupes often exhibit just such mindless loyalty.[2]

VERSE 21a. With biting irony Paul said that if those are the characteristics of true apostles, then he must acknowledge that he and his associates

2. For example, the followers of Rev. Jim Jones in the notorious Jonestown, Guyana.

had been too weak to qualify (cf. 10:10; 12). The NIV catches the thought well: "To my shame I admit that we were too weak for that!"

2. Paul's personal heritage and sufferings (11:21b-33)

VERSE 21b. The apostle now came to the actual presentation of his own boasts, the matter which he had been leading up to. He hesitated to do it—it made him feel like a fool—but circumstances had forced him. He would compare himself to the various characteristics of which the false apostles continually boasted.

VERSE 22. "Are they Hebrews?" Paul asked. This term was used in several ways.[3] It primarily meant persons of Jewish descent. Secondarily, it could denote Jews of Palestinian origin, as distinct from Diaspora Jews.[4] At the very least, Paul was here saying that even though the false apostles claimed to be Jewish, he was no less a Jew than they were. Perhaps the claim went beyond mere nationality to the more restricted connotation of a Palestinian origin. Even here Paul was not inferior, for although he had been born in Tarsus of Cilicia, he had been reared in Jerusalem (Acts 22:3). "Israelites" also identified the false apostles as Jewish, but emphasizes the nation as the chosen people of God. "Seed of Abraham" (KJV) calls attention to the messianic promise and the covenant which God had given. In all of these designations Paul was not inferior to his enemies in any respect.

VERSE 23. The question, "Are they servants of Christ?" begins a new thought in which Paul showed his proofs that he was Christ's servant in a far higher sense than any of these false apostles could claim. The question did not imply that these men were actually Christ's servants. In fact Paul had just called them Satan's servants (11:14-15). He merely repeated their claim, perhaps with some irony.

As Paul insisted on his superiority to the false apostles, he used an even stronger term[5] than "fool" (verses 16, 17, 21). This time he felt beserk for

3. Walter Gutbrod, "Hebraios," TDNT, III, 389-391.

4. Diaspora refers to non-Palestinian Jews, whose residence in the Gentile world and use of the Greek language tended to set them somewhat apart from their Palestinian brothers.

5. The earlier terms in the passage are *aphrōn* (11:16) and *aphrosunē* (11:17, 21). In 11:23 it is *paraphroneō*, "to be beside oneself, mad, insane."

speaking this way. The NASB ("I speak as if insane") and NIV ("I am out of my mind to talk like this") have conveyed the thought well.

The evidence Paul presented that he was Christ's servant is overwhelming. His labors had been more strenuous, prolonged, and widespread than the imposters' work. Although we do not have records of all of Paul's activities, or any records of the false apostles, the information we do have regarding Paul gives no reason to doubt this claim. He had been in prison more than these enemies. By the time of this writing, his only recorded imprisonment was at Philippi (Acts 16:23). Apparently he had others not mentioned in Acts. He had been beaten "times without number." Frequently he had been in situations where the risk of death was very great. Acts records such instances at Damascus (9:23), Pisidian Antioch (13:50), Iconium (14:5-6), Lystra (14:19), Philippi (16:19-40), Thessalonica (17:5-9), and Berea (17:13).

VERSE 24. On five occasions, none of them recorded in Scripture, Paul had received the Jewish punishment of thirty-nine lashes. Mosaic law (Deut. 25:1-3) prescribed a maximum of forty blows. As carried out by the synagogues, this was traditionally limited to thirty-nine so as not to exceed the legal limit.

VERSE 25. Three times Paul had been given the Gentile punishment of a beating with rods. Only one of these was recorded in Acts—the incident at Philippi (Acts 16:22-23). Although a Roman citizen was exempt from this, sometimes the punishment was inflicted before the victim had a chance to claim his citizenship (Acts 16:37). The one episode of stoning is recounted in Acts 14:19. The three shipwrecks mentioned here are not mentioned elsewhere in the Bible (the shipwreck described in Acts 27 occurred after this writing). However, Paul had made at least seven voyages, probably eight or nine, and possibly even more by this time,[6] and could easily have

6. Paul's voyages (recorded in Acts, prior to the time he wrote II Corinthians) included: Caesarea to Tarsus (Acts 9:30; Gal. 1:21); Tarsus to Antioch (Acts 11:25-26; possibly overland); Seleucia to Salamis (Acts 13:4); Paphos to Perga (Acts 13:13); Attalia to Antioch (Acts 14:25-26); Troas to Neapolis (Acts 16:11); Berea to Athens (Acts 17:14-15; possibly overland); Corinth to Ephesus (Acts 18:18-19); Ephesus to Caesarea (Acts 18:21-22). In addition, the "painful visit" to Corinth could have required more sea travel.

experienced this. In one of those calamitous shipwrecks he had spent a day and night adrift before rescue or landing occurred.

VERSE 26. The frequent journeys were not pleasant excursions but dangerous travels, as the Book of Acts reveals. Swollen rivers caused real peril. Robbers were a threat to any ancient traveler. Danger hounded Paul's steps, both from persecuting Jews (Acts 9:23, 29; 13:50; 14:5, 19; 17:5, 13; 18:12; I Thess. 2:15) and from Gentiles (Iconium, Acts 14:2-5; Philippi, 16:19-22; and Ephesus, 19:23-41). Whether he was in city or desert, or at sea, he faced continual danger in pursuing his service for Christ. There were dangers at sea other than shipwreck (see Acts 20:3) which had been previously mentioned. One of the threats he faced was posed by false brethren. Perhaps he had in mind Judaizing opponents who were bitter against him and did not hesitate to stir up Christians against him, and may even have reported him to authorities if it would remove him from the scene.

VERSE 27. "Labor and hardship" was an expression Paul had used when discussing his manual labor at Thessalonica (I Thess. 2:9; II Thess. 3:8). "In watchings often" (KJV) probably refers to the sleepless nights he endured, working late to support himself so he would not burden the church. "Hunger and thirst" were sometimes his experience when his own labors did not fully supply his needs. "In fastings often" (KJV) does not seem to refer here to ritualistic fasts (he was talking about suffering, not devotion), but to those times when food ran out altogether, or when other circumstances made eating impossible. He also knew what it was to have insufficient clothing, especially when traveling on long journeys when nights were cold and accommodations primitive.

VERSE 28. Apart from the things mentioned, which were burdensome enough, Paul carried still another responsibility which none of the false apostles shared. He bore the daily pressure of concern about the churches which looked to him for help. This was the greatest of his burdens. All of the churches he had founded were constantly besieging him with problems of all sorts. Nor were they minor matters, as the contents of Paul's letters make clear. It was a never-ending burden that was made heavier by the other hardships just enumerated.

VERSE 29. Paul's sense of responsibility for the churches made him sympathetic to every struggling and suffering Christian of whom he was aware. The question, "Who is weak and I am not weak?" (KJV) implies that Paul entered in fully with the weaknesses of the brethren and took them to his own heart. The previous recitation of his troubles and hardships made it clear that he was no stranger to personal misfortune. Thus he could readily sympathize with those experiencing some kind of weakness.

The second question, "Who is led into sin, and I do not inwardly burn?" (NIV) expresses either Paul's burning with shame and remorse along with the sinner over such a happening, or perhaps his indignation at the one who had seduced the victim. It may be that Paul experienced both of these feelings. His point was that his concern for the churches ran deep and added to the heavy load he carried.

VERSE 30. "If I must boast" (NIV) gives still another indication of Paul's reluctance at this whole aspect of the discussion. He did not enjoy these personal references, but was convinced that the situation demanded it. Consequently, he proceeded, but emphasized not his astounding achievements but his "weakness." By so doing, he showed the power of God who used him despite all of the troubles here enumerated. All of the glory thus will go to God, and Paul could hardly be accused of glorifying himself.

VERSE 31. This solemn assertion of the truthfulness of Paul's words refers primarily to the preceding discussion, although it is equally applicable to what follows, inasmuch as the "boasting" continues. The recitation of these tremendous labors and sufferings might seem incredible, but Paul insisted that his account was no exaggeration, and he wrote the account with the full consciousness that the omniscient God was a witness to his words.

The description of God as "blessed forever" (NASB, KJV) was common Hebrew terminology, and Paul also used it in Romans 1:25 and 9:5.

VERSE 32. The incident of Paul's escape from Damascus is mentioned also in Acts 9:23–25. Many scholars have found it puzzling that Paul should relate it here after the summation he had just given in 11:31. If the precise elements of the criticism Paul had faced were more fully known, the reasons for mention would doubtless be clear. Perhaps the false apostles had used the account of this undignified departure from Damascus to show his lack of apostolic stature. If so, Paul set the matter straight, explaining it as an outstanding example of apostolic suffering and deliverance from almost certain death.

Aretas IV was king of the Nabateans, whose capital was Petra. He ruled for thirty-one years, beginning in A.D. 9. The governor ("ethnarch," NASB) was an official appointed by Aretas, apparently to oversee a particular ethnic segment of the population. Damascus was not actually a Nabatean city at this time, but a colony of Nabateans may have lived in Damascus and may have been instigators of the plot against Paul.[7] Somehow the Jews were able to enlist the ethnarch's support in attempting to seize Paul.

VERSE 33. Although the city gates were being watched (Acts 9:24), Paul's friends made use of a window in the city wall, and lowered him to the ground outside by means of a basket. The term for "basket" (*sarganē*) emphasizes the fact that it was woven. It was probably made of rope or wicker. Once again Paul had "boasted" of something which superficial viewers would call weakness. Yet Paul saw his escape as a demonstration of God's provision for His appointed messenger, even though his escape showed human frailty and humiliation.

3. Paul's revelations from the Lord (12:1-10)

VERSE 1. Once again Paul claimed that this "boasting" was necessary. He had been driven to it by his opponents, although it was quite distasteful to him and he would gain no personal advantage from it.

Paul now shifted a bit from enumerating his sufferings to talking about "visions and revelations." However, he soon returned to that former theme as he explained the "thorn in the flesh" which resulted from this revelation. "Visions" were visual experiences which God provided. "Revelations" were the truths which God imparted, including those conveyed in visions. Were the impostors claiming special visions? Or did Paul mention his vision

7. An excellent resumé of the historical evidence and of various analyses of the problem is given by E. M. Blaiklock, "Aretas," *The Zondervan Pictorial Encyclopedia of the Bible,* I, 299-300.

because he knew it was an experience which they could not equal? Whatever the immediate reason, the following account is remarkable in its own right, and Paul's evaluation of it reveals much about his character.

VERSE 2. "I know a man in Christ." The verb should be translated as a present (not "I knew," as though he no longer knows this person, KJV). The third person is used, but it is clear from verse 7 that Paul was talking about himself. His reluctance to boast about himself probably caused him to describe the incident in this indirect way.

"Fourteen years ago" would date the occurrence in A.D. 41 or 42, during Paul's years in Tarsus (see time chart, Fig. 1). Efforts to identify the incident with his conversion on the road to Damascus, his trance in Jerusalem, the stoning at Lystra, or any other known event in Paul's career cannot be harmonized with the best chronological data.

In this remarkable experience Paul did not know whether he was actually in his body, as Enoch and Elijah, and had been temporarily "raptured" (the same word is used for the eschatological rapture of the church), or whether he had died and was without his mortal body. Inasmuch as Paul himself did not know, it is fruitless for us to speculate. At the same time, it reminds us that his ability to function in the "third heaven" did not depend on having an earthly body. He was not conscious of having a body (if indeed he had it), nor did he miss it (if he did not have it).

The "third heaven" is later equated with paradise (v. 4) and refers to the dwelling place of God. Scripture itself reflects nothing of the idea of seven heavens as found in extrabiblical Jewish literature and other writings. It is not certain, therefore, whether Paul had in mind a threefold division of atmospheric, stellar, and divine heavens, or whether he simply meant by "third" the highest heaven (Heb. 7:26).

VERSE 3. The solemn assertion of verse 2 is repeated as Paul moved further into his description of this remarkable event.

VERSE 4. Inasmuch as verses 3 and 4 belong together, it is best to regard the statement not as describing a second experience, but as the same as mentioned in verse 2 with a new detail added, namely, the hearing of some inexpressible words. The words were intelligible, but Paul was not permitted to repeat them. Apparently their purpose was intended for Paul alone, and although they made a profound impression on him, he never communicated their content to others.

"Paradise" would seem to be identical with "the third heaven" (v. 2). The term occurs two other times in the New Testament. Jesus promised the penitent thief that he would be with Him in paradise (Luke 23:43), the place of the righteous dead. The tree of life is located in the paradise of God (Rev. 2:7). In the present passage "Paradise" denotes heaven, God's dwelling place. In all three it apparently refers to that place where God resides, where all the dead in Christ presently are awaiting resurrection.

VERSE 5. Paul was willing to boast in "such a man," that is, "a man in Christ" (12:2), because God was fully responsible for all the actions and would get the glory. But apart from those God-produced experiences, he would not glory in his accomplishments except in the obvious weaknesses which God had been able to surmount.

VERSE 6. Any boasting Paul would ever do would be based squarely on facts. He would not be so foolish as to talk about himself as though personal accomplishments and perhaps exaggerated claims would gain him a greater following. Therefore, he even refrained from a conservative, factual sort of boasting lest a wrong impression be gained. He wanted no one to elevate him beyond the realm of ordinary humans on the basis of his boasting about his unique revelations. He preferred to let his followers base their conclusions on what they saw him do or heard him teach. By stressing his weaknesses, rather than his unusual privileges, God rather than the man would get the credit.

VERSE 7. Paul acknowledged the possibility that pride could have asserted itself in him because of his vision. Therefore, God allowed Satan to buffet him (literally, "to strike with the fist") through something Paul called a "thorn in the flesh."[8] Apparently the "thorn" was a chronic affliction that served as a reminder to Paul that he was still an ordinary mortal, dependent on God for the strength to fulfill his mission. Efforts to

8. The word *skolops* can also mean "stake," and some scholars have interpreted the metaphor as an impaling or crucifixion of the apostle. However, the meaning "thorn" is common in the papyri and also in the LXX, and thus seems more likely here.

identify Paul's "thorn" have not reached a consensus. Some commentators explain "flesh" as his human nature, and suggest such things as sensual passion as the "thorn." It is more common to regard "flesh" here as the physical body (as in Gal. 4:13), and explain the "thorn" as an ailment such as epilepsy, headaches, eye disease, or malaria. Whatever its precise nature, Paul regarded it as caused by Satan but allowed by God and used by Him to accomplish an important purpose. Job 2:5-6 and Luke 13:16 describe other instances where Satan caused physical infirmity.

VERSE 8. Paul had been understandably distressed by this thorn,[9] and prayed that God would remove it. Apparently the answer did not come until after the third request, a reminder that persevering prayer has great value. The incident also demonstrated the fact that earnest and believing prayer for healing of physical ailments (or anything else, for that matter) does not always result in removal of the affliction. It is assumed that Paul's praying was done in the biblical spirit of "Thy will be done," and thus he regarded God's response as a true answer, whether the specific request was granted or denied.

VERSE 9. When the answer came, it was, "My grace is sufficient for you, for power [of Christ] is perfected in weakness." Divine favor always furnishes enough power to see His servants through their distresses, and this power is displayed most conspicuously in the presence of human weakness. It is not known how early in this fourteen-year-period Paul received the answer. By his use of the Greek perfect tense, "He has said," it is clear that Paul recognized God's explanation as still in effect. Even though it may have occurred many years ago, Paul had accepted it and endured the thorn without despair or bitterness.

Paul's wholehearted acceptance of the divine will in this matter is seen in his exultant testimony. He would most gladly accept physical weakness in order for Christ's power to occupy and energize him more fully. It was

9. Some scholars suggest that *toutou* ("this") refers to "messenger of Satan" rather than to "thorn," and hence translate "that he should depart from me." However, "messenger of Satan" is merely appositional with "thorn," and it is therefore better to regard "thorn" as the main idea and the antecedent of "this."

certainly not the most pleasant way to live, and Paul never adopted an ascetic philosophy which courted suffering for its own sake. But he accepted his thorn with good grace because it enabled others to see in his accomplishments the power of Christ operating with outstanding success in a vessel that was greatly hampered by a "thorn in the flesh." Paul would rather have the power of Christ resting on him than to have relief from suffering. What exemplary dedication!

VERSE 10. Because this commitment had mastered him, Paul could actually welcome weaknesses, insults, distresses, persecutions, and difficulties for Christ's sake. They key was "for Christ's sake." Only when these afflictions came in his line of duty as Christ's apostle could he actually take pleasure in them. His natural inclinations were far different, as would be true of any normal person. He had learned, however, by God's answer to his thrice-asked prayer and by the experiences of his apostleship that his personal weakness could be superseded by the strength of Christ. This made him equal to his task.

4. Paul's "signs of an apostle" (12:11-13)

VERSE 11. As Paul neared the end of this section about boasting, he acknowledged once again that he felt foolish in recounting this personal data. He had done it only because he felt compelled to by the Corinthians and the situation they had allowed to develop in their church. In view of all that Paul had done at Corinth, the Corinthians themselves should have rallied to Paul's defense when the false apostles began exerting their influence. Because the Corinthians had kept silent and permitted Paul to be grossly misrepresented, even to the point where the gospel message itself was threatened, he had been forced to speak up for himself.

Again Paul asserted that he was in no way inferior to the "super-apostles" (NIV; see also 11:5, 13). The reference is to the false apostles who made superior claims for themselves and sought to discredit Paul. "Even though I am nothing" was Paul's disclaimer of personal credit or glory. Whatever he was personally resulted from God's grace. Officially, however, he was far superior to those intruders, as the Corinthian believers should have easily recognized.

VERSE 12. The proof of Paul's claim was that "the signs of an apostle" (KJV) had been performed in their midst when he had been with them. These had been done even during adverse circumstances when patience was necessary. The phrase "signs and wonders and miracles" describes miraculous acts from various standpoints—as credentials or proofs, as awe-inspiring deeds, and as displays of divine power. Although the Book of Acts does not record any miracles at Corinth, apparently there were some. The fact that performance of miracles was a sign or credential of a true apostle is corroborated by the promise given to the Eleven in Mark 16:14-18.

VERSE 13. Apparently part of the slander was that Paul's ministry at Corinth was not equal to that in other churches founded by apostles, and thus the Corinthians were being made to feel cheated. Paul had been answering this charge throughout this letter by pointing to the kind of ministry he continually exercised. He had pointed out that the credentials of a true apostle had been displayed by his miracles, his preaching the truth of Christ, his demonstrating of Christ's power in his own weaknesses, and by the transformed lives of the Corinthians themselves.

With playful humor and perhaps a touch of irony, Paul suggested that the only respect in which the Corinthians had been slighted as recipients of his ministry was his failure to let them pay him. "Forgive me this wrong" should have caused some wry smiles. Certainly the Corinthians did not regard this as a wrong for Paul to forego his rights in order to make things easier for them.

Thus ends Paul's "boasting." Painful though it may have been for him, the thoughtful reader recognizes that the apostle was a most uncommon man. His commitment to the cause of Christ in spite of incredible hardship has continued to challenge millions of Christians in all the centuries since.

Questions for Discussion

1. What safeguards did Paul use to prevent his boasting from becoming self-glorification?

2. Why did Paul use indirect methods to describe the man who was caught up to the third heaven?
3. Why do you think Paul "heard inexpressible words" in the third heaven if he could not tell about them?
4. Why was Paul not given release from his thorn in the flesh?
5. What truths can be learned about prayer from Paul's experience regarding his thorn?

13

A Third Visit to Corinth

II Corinthians 12:14—13:14

A crucial part of an emotional letter is its concluding portion. Whether it will be accepted and will motivate the readers to appropriate action, or will simply irritate them and thus compound the problem, may depend on the tone of the final paragraphs. Paul had been writing about some sensitive matters. He had spoken of misunderstandings, mistreatment, wrong interpretations placed on his actions, and of a disturbing tendency at Corinth to tolerate wrong teaching. If his apostolic admonitions were to be heeded, Paul must make every attempt to leave the impression that he was the Corinthians' friend and sought only their best interests.

Paul also wished to insure that he would be welcomed when he came to Corinth on his next visit. Fostering a good spirit among the Corinthians was not just an official concern that their problems be solved. Paul desired that his personal relationships with them be completely restored, and that no awkwardness or embarrassment mar his coming visit.

The letter had said some stern things, but this did not mean that Paul had any less love for his readers. His heart was still opened wide toward them (6:11). The next paragraphs set forth his plans, and revealed the feelings of the apostle as he contemplated seeing them once again.

C. *Paul's Proposed Third Visit (12:14—13:10)*

1. A promise not to be burdensome (12:14-18)

VERSE 14. This was the third visit Paul would be making to Corinth (as clearly indicated in 13:1). The first visit resulted in the founding of the church (Acts 18). The second was an unrecorded "painful visit" (2:1, NIV), presumably following the writing of I Corinthians. Now he was ready to visit once again.

Paul promised not to be a burden to the church when he came. He would continue his policy of refusing support from the church. Even the accusations over this matter which he had been answering would not cause him to change his mind. His reason was that he wanted to leave no misunderstanding over the issue of personal gain. Paul did not want to acquire the Corinthians' possessions but their souls for Christ. He desired their spiritual growth. Even though the sharing of one's goods with others can be a spiritual act, those who are spiritually immature often view it from a materialistic aspect. To avoid this problem, Paul had adopted his financial policy, even though he had a right to accept support from those to whom he ministered (I Cor. 9:11, 14, 15, 18).

To illustrate his procedure, Paul used the analogy of parents and their children. It is the obligation of parents to care for their minor children, rather than the reverse. Likewise Paul felt it appropriate, as the spiritual father of the Corinthian believers, to labor for them and not expect them to support him.

VERSE 15. As their father, therefore, Paul would most gladly "spend and be spent" (KJV) for the welfare of his spiritual children. This surely went beyond the expenditure of money (that is, supporting himself rather than accepting pay) to the expenditure of himself in time, energy, concern, and anything else which would assist their well-being. Then came the plaintive question, "If I love you the more, am I to be loved the less?" Past experience seemed to say that the more he extended himself, the more he was criticized and misjudged. Was that to continue? Sensitive readers hope that was not the case.

VERSE 16. "Be that as it may" (NASB; literally, "but let it be") indicated that Paul had said all he intended to on that subject. He had not burdened the Corinthians with his support, and they knew it. No further evidence was needed.

"Crafty fellow that I am, I took you in by deceit." This is probably another of the slanderous reports that had circulated about Paul in Corinth. Inasmuch as he obviously had taken no payment from the church, the false apostles may have suggested that this was merely a device to hide the fact that he was somehow profiting from the collection being raised for Jerusalem. Of course, Paul was admitting no such thing, but was using some of the language of his accusers.

VERSE 17. Paul was closing all the loopholes whereby his detractors might plant doubts among the Corinthians. The false apostles could not find evidence of wrongdoing by Paul. Yet the fact that he served without pay was so incomprehensible to them that they felt certain that he must be receiving compensation somehow. Paul knew that his emissaries would be suspected of collusion with him, especially since they were involved in the financial matter of the collection. The question expected a negative answer, as NASB reflects accurately in translation.[1] The Corinthian church knew quite well that none of Paul's assistants had made a profit from the church, nor had they been channels to convey funds to Paul.

VERSE 18. More specifically mention is made of Titus and a certain brother (literally, "the brother") who had been to Corinth. Paul was sufficiently confident of their exemplary conduct to have no qualms about how the Corinthians would answer a question involving financial irregularities.[2] "The brother" is not otherwise identified, although he may be the same as mentioned in 8:18 or the one in 8:22. The original readers, of course, understood who was meant because he had been with them.

Titus had been to Corinth on at least two occasions prior to the present trip in which he would deliver the epistle. He had initiated the collection (8:6), apparently prior to the writing of I Corinthians, inasmuch as the collection was known at that time (I Cor. 16:1-4). He had also been at

1. The question is introduced by *mē*.
2. This question is also introduced by *mēti*, indicating a negative answer expected.

Corinth more recently, perhaps to deliver the severe letter, and had met Paul in Macedonia with a report of good news (7:5-16). Now Titus was going back to Corinth, presumably as the bearer of II Corinthians. The present trip would be for the purpose of completing the collection, and would be made in the company of *two* other Christian brothers (8:6, 18, 22). This mention in 12:18 of Titus and *one* other brother is most likely a reference to one of the earlier visits by Titus.

On that past occasion, the Corinthians would certainly admit that no suspicion had arisen over the actions of Titus and his companion. They had shown the same attitude[3] in their dealings at Corinth as Paul had done. They had also followed Paul's example so far as their actions were concerned. Both Paul and his assistants conducted themselves in a way that was above reproach. None of them had been a burden to the Corinthian church.

2. Misgivings about his visit (12:19-21)

VERSE 19. It is not certain whether the first clause should be treated as a question (KJV, NIV) or a declaration (NASB). If it be regarded as a question, then the approach is a bit more delicate. Paul was not actually accusing the Corinthians of misunderstanding this letter (a circumstance he could not know as yet), but by asking the question he prompted the readers to examine their own responses. There was a distinct possibility that his readers supposed he was answering his opponents merely in order to protect himself.

The truth was that Paul regarded himself as laboring under the watchful eye of God and as a man in Christ (see the similar statement in 2:17). His purpose in writing was to protect and nurture the spiritual life of the Corinthians. He did not regard the Corinthians as his judges whom he needed to appease, but as pupils whom he desired to teach. He expressed a similar thought in I Corinthians 4:3-4.

---

3. The term *pneumati* could conceivably be regarded as "Spirit," referring to the Holy Spirit. Most interpreters treat it as "spirit" or "attitude," consistent with the parallelism in the next question.

VERSE 20. In contemplating his forthcoming visit, Paul had several misgivings. He was fearful (but not certain) that his hopes regarding rectification of the Corinthians' problems may have been premature. Titus' report had greatly encouraged him, but the harsh realities of an on-site visit might provide a disappointing letdown.

Paul was also aware that if the problems he might encounter on his arrival required him to act with sternness, this would not be welcomed by the Corinthians. The possibility existed of a mutual disappointment when his visit occurred.

Specific instances are cited to illustrate the potential problems. Eight items, perhaps grouped as four pairs, suggest the types of situations which Paul suspected might still be present at Corinth. Strife and jealousy describe the quarreling and envy which had been prevalent at Corinth. Displays of anger and selfish ambition easily develop when problems fester and unworthy leaders exploit them. Evil speakings and whisperings describe the slanders, gossiping, innuendoes, and talebearing which keep a church in turmoil if its problems are not settled. Arrogance and disturbances depict the "swellings [of pride]" (KJV; *phusiōseis*)[4] that ultimately cause all kinds of disorder.

VERSE 21. Another of Paul's fears was the possibility that God would humiliate him in the Corinthians' presence if he found their problems uncorrected. Paul took very personally the difficulties of the Corinthian believers, and it would be a humbling experience for him if he saw that much of his labor had gone for nothing. He would mourn over those who had sinned and had not repented. The sins enumerated here are different from the jealousies and strife mentioned in 12:20. These seem to be largely instances of immorality, such as were denounced at considerable length in I Corinthians. This may account for the statement that they had sinned "in the past" (NASB), "earlier" (NIV), or "already" (KJV).[5] "Uncleanness" (KJV) depicts the impurity of the sin. "Fornication" (KJV) describes sexual

4. From the root *phusioō*, "to blow up, puff up, inflate."

5. The Greek participle *proēmartēkotōn* incorporates the temporal idea in the prepositional prefix.

promiscuity, including prostitution—a social problem rampant at Corinth. "Sensuality" (NASB) looks at the same sins from the standpoint of the wantonness and excess of the conduct. The passage implies that those involved had been previously confronted in Paul's letters and visits, and had been given opportunity to repent. Continuing refusal to do so would reveal a hardened heart, and would call for severe discipline.

3. A warning of discipline when he comes (13:1-4)

VERSE 1. This "third time" Paul was coming should be understood in terms of three actual visits, not merely intended ones, or a combination of visits and letters. He had been at Corinth on two previous occasions—the founding visit (Acts 18), and the painful visit (2:1)—and the forthcoming visit would be the third.

Paul quoted a well-known Old Testament passage to show that his dealings with offenders at Corinth would be done with proper witnesses (Deut. 19:15; cf. Deut. 18:16; I Tim. 5:19). He would not take matters into his own hands, but would make certain that strict propriety would be maintained in every instance of discipline. The reference to "three witnesses" in close proximity to the mention of Paul's "third" coming leads some to imagine that the apostle regarded his comings as three separate testimonies fulfilling the Old Testament requirement. It is extremely unlikely, however, that Paul imagined that testimony coming from one person (himself) on three different occasions satisfied the intent (and usual meaning) of the quoted passage. The explanation given above is therefore preferable.

VERSE 2. The translation in KJV is awkward, and one should consult NASB or NIV for a clearer rendering. Paul had already warned the church of this impending action when he had made his second or "painful visit." He repeated the warning just before his third visit. The warning was to those who had "sinned in the past," that is, the ones described in 12:21, and also to "all the rest." The latter may have referred to others who may have been wrongly influenced by the original group and were now also deserving of disciplinary action. On his previous visit, Paul had said, "If I come again, I will not spare." The "if" was now about to be realized. Sufficient time had elapsed for these sins in the church to be dealt with. If they had not, no more delay could be expected.

VERSE 3. This verse is grammatically a part of the preceding one. Because the Corinthians had been led to doubt Paul's authority, and thus to act in contradiction to Christ's instruction, he would be forced to speak severely when he came. The Corinthians would certainly recognize at that time that the very authority of Christ would display itself through him. Paul reminded his readers of their own experience of Christ, for His power had been amply demonstrated in their lives. Christ's might had been witnessed in the miracles they had seen (12:12), as well as in the spiritual victories of transformed lives in the wicked city of Corinth. Hence when Paul would come again and be unsparing in his dealings with persistent offenders, the powerful proof which they sought of his divine authorization would be evident. They might not welcome it, however, as much as they thought.

VERSE 4. If it bothered the Corinthians that Paul did not always behave as a powerful, authoritarian leader, let them remember that Christ also had displayed this combination of weakness and strength. He had shown "weakness" by human estimation when he submitted meekly to His enemies without violence or retaliation, and endured the humiliation of crucifixion. That was not the whole story, however, for He also was resurrected by the power of God, showing that His "weakness" was no permanent nor degrading condition.

Inasmuch as believers are in union with Christ, they also demonstrate at various times both the weakness of nonretaliation against opponents and the resurrection power of God in performing His commands. Because of the context, it is likely that "we shall live with Him" does not refer to the future resurrection but to the demonstration of our present union with Christ in His resurrection whereby we walk in newness of life (Rom. 6:4). As applied to the immediate situation, Paul referred to his forthcoming visit in which he would not be weakly submissive but would firmly display the power of God in dealing with those who opposed His truth.

4. A challenge to examine themselves (13:5-10)

VERSE 5. The word "yourselves" is emphatic in both statements; the idea is, "Yourselves be testing . . . yourselves be proving." Paul was aware that the Corinthians had been clamoring for him to prove himself (13:3). They should have been more concerned about themselves.

Paul asked the Corinthians to test themselves regarding "the faith," that is, the Christian faith. Were they true Christians? Did they really recognize that Christ Jesus was dwelling in them and had brought new life? Surely they would acknowledge these things to be true. The only alternative was to fail the test, and Paul did not consider this at all likely. The reason why he challenged the Corinthians to examine the validity of their participation in the Christian faith is explained in the next statement.

VERSE 6. If the Corinthians would concur that they were a genuine part of the household of faith—and how could they do otherwise?—they should be hard-pressed to deny that Christ was speaking in the one who had brought them to faith! Consequently a recognition of the evidence that Christ was in them should also make them sensitive to the same evidence that Christ was in Paul. If they passed the test of their own scrutiny, so should Paul.

VERSE 7. Paul's prayer was that the Corinthians might rectify their conduct in all respects. He and his associates did not want to act as disciplinarians when they came. They would much prefer to see the evidence that true spiritual growth was taking place in the Corinthians' lives. Paul's desire was not primarily vindication of himself and his helpers ("not that we ourselves should appear approved"), although that would certainly be one result if the Corinthians complied fully with his counsel. His real aim was the spiritual development of the Corinthians themselves, irrespective of what it may have implied for Paul. "Even though we should appear unapproved" probably refers to the possibility that Paul and his helpers would lose their opportunity to speak severely and thus display a "proof" of apostolic authority (13:3). Nevertheless, Paul was quite willing to appear less lordly if it meant that the Corinthians were progressing.

VERSE 8. It is possible to regard this statement as somewhat proverbial, "we can do nothing against the truth, but only for the truth." If it is so regarded, Paul is understood to say that ultimately the truth (or perhaps God's will or the Christian faith) will prevail and man cannot permanently thwart it. Probably, however, the statement had a direct reference to Paul's

ministry and his intentions. His apostleship was for the purpose of further-
ing the Christian cause, not hindering it. He was totally committed to
winning people to Christ and fostering their spiritual growth. Whatever
was required to accomplish this goal he was willing to do, whether it meant
dealing sternly on occasion (and thus displaying firm authority), or
seeming to be mild-mannered and unobtrusive without the trappings of
power which some people were associating with leadership. Personal
vindication for its own sake was meaningless to Paul. It was the truth
which concerned him, not his reputation.

VERSE 9. Therefore, Paul could rejoice whenever the situation in the
churches was healthy. When the church at Corinth showed itself to be
"strong" in the sense of spiritual maturity in dealing with sin and rejecting
false teachers, then Paul and the other apostles were happy to desist from
displays of strong authority. Being "weak" in that sense was no disgrace.
Rather, it was an indication that things were going well. Paul found no
pleasure in figuratively wielding a club. In fact, he was praying for this
matter of their restoration. "Perfection" (KJV, NIV) or "made complete"
(NASB) translates a word (*katartisin*) that occurs only here in the New
Testament. Some of its cognates convey the idea of restoring, mending,
equipping, bringing to a suitable state, or making complete. The apostle's
concern was not to show power, but to mend broken lives and bring them
to an appropriate level of Christian maturity.

VERSE 10. It was with this goal in mind that Paul was writing the present
letter. He had been very direct, almost blunt, to accomplish his purpose.
The reason was to avoid a personal confrontation when he made his visit.
His memories of the painful visit must have been vivid, and a repetition was
to be avoided if at all possible. He hoped that the letter would finalize what
Titus' recent visit had begun, and that full restoration of harmony toward
each other and toward him would be the result. He would not hesitate to
use the sterner aspects of his authority if some persisted in evil ways (13:2),
but the ultimate purpose of his God-given authority as an apostle was for
building the Corinthians up, not tearing them down (he had told them the
same thing in 10:8). Even if severe treatment became necessary for a time,
it was only for the purpose of making greater growth possible. But if they

profited from this epistle, the forthcoming visit could be far more pleasant.

Did this letter achieve its purpose? Christian readers sincerely hope so, although direct evidence is lacking. Murray J. Harris has suggested several indications that it was successful.[6] First, Romans was written after Paul arrived at Corinth on this visit, and no particular difficulties are reflected. Second, his plans to visit Rome and then Spain would hardly have been so well-formed if the church from which he was writing was in complete disarray. Third, the Corinthians did complete the collection as Paul was urging (Rom. 15:26-27). Fourth, the preservation of II Corinthians by that congregation argues for the acceptance of Paul's mission.

V. Final Greeting (13:11-14)

A. Concluding Exhortations (13:11)

VERSE 11. Those who question the unity of II Corinthians usually treat 13:11-14 as the conclusion to chapters 1-9. This commentator, however, sees no need for such radical dissection, and understands this portion to follow naturally with a more positive concluding note after the severe warning of the preceding section.

Whether the translation "rejoice" (NASB) is preferable to "farewell" (KJV; cf. "goodby," NIV) is debatable. Both are legitimate renderings of the Greek word. "Farewell" is surely appropriate at the end of a letter. Furthermore, it may be less startling to the readers after the stern warning that Paul would not spare them when he came again. Asking the readers to "rejoice" after such a warning sounds a bit abrupt. On the other hand, "rejoice" is used elsewhere as a Pauline exhortation at the end of his letters (Phil. 4:4; I Thess. 5:16). If this is the sense here, Paul was enjoining them to find real joy in the Lord, and cease their present critical attitudes.

"Be made complete" is a command using the verb that is cognate to the noun in 13:9. Paul had prayed that this completeness or restoration might occur, but the Corinthians themselves could assist the accomplishment by

6. Murray J. Harris, "2 Corinthians," *The Expositor's Bible Commentary,* X, 404-405.

submitting to God's guidance and Paul's instruction. "Be comforted" may be telling the Corinthians not to lose heart over the past situation, but to be encouraged by the amount of rectification already achieved and look forward to better days ahead. It is possible, however, to translate the verb as "let yourselves be exhorted," that is, "listen to my exhortation." If this was Paul's meaning, he was urging his readers to heed his advice.

"Be of one mind" (KJV) is, literally, "be minding the same thing." This was not a demand for absence of individuality, but a plea for unity arising out of the essential principles of Christian action. "Live in peace" is an exhortation which would be easy to follow if the preceding admonitions were heeded. Peace is one of the fruits which the Holy Spirit will produce if believers cease putting up hindrances (Gal. 5:22).

The five imperatives are followed by the promise that the God of love and peace will be with believers. This encouragement was a reminder that these exhortations did not place an intolerable burden on the church to achieve success by its unaided efforts. To the contrary, the apostolic counsel would be energized by God Himself who would produce a greater love and a resultant peace among them if they would let Him.

B. Greetings (13:12-13)

VERSE 12. The exhortation to greet with a holy kiss occurs five times in the New Testament (Rom. 16:16; I Cor. 16:20; II Cor. 13:12; I Thess. 5:26; I Peter 5:14). This sort of greeting was the common one between members of the same sex in the ancient world. In believers' encounters with one another, their greetings should be wholesome and genuine, not with a hypocritical sign of love followed by a critical spirit toward their brethren. Very early in the church, the holy kiss was incorporated into ceremonial usage. In the second century Justin Martyr wrote of its usage in connection with the Eucharist.[7] It was apparently intended to indicate the brotherhood that existed in the family of God. Unfortunately, the practice was sometimes abused.

7. Justin Martyr, "The First Apology" (chap. 65), in *The Fathers of the Church*, VI, 105.

VERSE 13.[8] "All the saints greet you." These would be the Macedonian Christians who were with Paul at the place of writing. These Christians could have been at Philippi, Thessalonica, or Berea. More precise identification cannot be given since the particular spot in Macedonia from which Paul wrote is not known to us. The reference to "all the saints" would serve as a reminder that a grand spiritual unity exists among all believers, which makes divisiveness and congregational disturbances inappropriate.

C. Benediction (13:14)

VERSE 14. The concluding benediction is the fullest of any with which Paul closed his epistles. This benediction is a beautiful trinitarian formula in a somewhat unusual order: Christ, God, Holy Spirit. It begins with Christ, whose gracious favor has made all the other benefits real in our lives. Inasmuch as "of the Lord Jesus Christ" is a subjective genitive here (that is, Christ's grace), it is likely that the remaining genitives in the formula are subjective also. Hence "the love of God" is His love for us (not our love for God) which needs to be recognized in the consciousness of all believers. "The fellowship of the Holy Spirit" (NASB, NIV) refers to the fellowship which the Spirit creates, first between believers and God, and then among believers toward each other. If the Corinthian church would heed the counsel of Paul as given in this letter, and would make itself available for receiving the blessing of this benediction, its problems would be quickly solved and its spiritual growth assured.

Questions for Discussion

1. What does this passage (12:14—13:10) imply about leadership styles?

---

8. In some versions, the sentence "all the saints greet you" is treated as part of verse 12. The remaining material is then numbered as verse 13, and there is no verse 14 (e.g., the *Berkeley Version in Modern English,* the *New American Bible,* the *New Testament in Modern English,* and *Today's English Version*). Whichever numbering scheme is followed, the same material is included.

2. How many times did Paul visit Corinth? What were those occasions?
3. From the content of II Corinthians, what do you conclude were some of the reasons why Paul's apostleship had been doubted at Corinth?
4. Should Christians today practice the holy kiss?
5. As you reflect on the entire letter of II Corinthians, what features impress you most?

Bibliography

Aldrich, Willard M. "The Objective Nature of the Reconciliation." *Bibliotheca Sacra* 118:469 (January 1961).

Arndt, W. F., and Gingrich, F. W. *A Greek-English Lexicon of the New Testament.* Chicago: University of Chicago Press, 1957.

Barrett, C. K. "Paul's Opponents in II Corinthians." *New Testament Studies* 17:3 (April 1971).

———. *The Second Epistle to the Corinthians.* New York: Harper & Row, Publishers, 1974.

Bernard, J. H. "Second Corinthians." In *Expositor's Greek Testament.* Grand Rapids: Wm. B. Eerdmans Publishing Co., 1952.

Blaiklock, E. M. "Aretas." In *The Zondervan Pictorial Encyclopedia of the Bible,* edited by Merrill C. Tenney. Grand Rapids: Zondervan Publishing House, 1975.

Boyer, James L. *For a World Like Ours.* Winona Lake, IN: BMH Books, 1971.

Broomall, Wick. "II Corinthians." In *Wycliffe Bible Commentary,* edited by Charles F. Pfeiffer and Everett F. Harrison. Chicago: Moody Press, 1962.

Cassidy, Ronald. "Paul's Attitude to Death in II Corinthians 5:1-10." *The Evangelical Quarterly,* vol. 43 (1971).

Chafer, Lewis Sperry. *Systematic Theology.* Dallas: Dallas Seminary Press, 1948.

Denney, James. "The Second Epistle to the Corinthians." In *The Expositor's Bible.* Grand Rapids: Wm. B. Eerdmans Publishing Co., reprinted 1943.

Egan, Rory B. "Lexical Evidence on Two Pauline Passages." *Novum Testamentum* 19:1 (January 1977).

Fee, Gordon D. "Charis in II Corinthians 1:15: Apostolic Parousia and Paul-Corinth Chronology." *New Testament Studies* 24:4 (July 1978).

———. "II Corinthians VI.14–VII.1 and Food Offered to Idols." *New Testament Studies* 23:2 (January 1977).

Fraser, John W. "Paul's Knowledge of Jesus: II Corinthians V.16 Once More." *New Testament Studies* 17:3 (April 1971).

Guthrie, Donald. *New Testament Introduction, The Pauline Epistles*. Chicago: Inter-Varsity Press, 1961.

Harris, Murray J. "2 Corinthians." In *The Expositor's Bible Commentary*, volume 10, edited by Frank E. Gaebelein. Grand Rapids: Zondervan Publishing House, 1976.

Harrison, Everett F. *Introduction to the New Testament*. Grand Rapids: Wm. B. Eerdmans Publishing Co., 1964.

Hickling, C. J. A. "The Sequence of Thought in II Corinthians, Chapter Three." *New Testament Studies* 21:3 (April 1975).

Hoyt, Samuel L. "The Judgment Seat of Christ and Unconfessed Sins." *Bibliotheca Sacra* 137:545 (January 1980).

———. "The Negative Aspects of the Christian's Judgment." *Bibliotheca Sacra* 137:546 (April 1980).

Hughes, Philip Edgecumbe. *Commentary on the Second Epistle to the Corinthians*. The New International Commentary series. Grand Rapids: Wm. B. Eerdmans Publishing Co., 1962.

Ironside, H. A. *Addresses on the Second Epistle to the Corinthians*. New York: Loizeaux Brothers, Publishers, n.d.

Jones, Montague Rhodes. *The Apocryphal New Testament*. Oxford: The Clarendon Press, reprinted 1969.

Justin Martyr. "The First Apology." Chapter 65 in *The Writings of Justin Martyr*, translated by Thomas B. Falls. The Fathers of the Church series. Washington, DC: Catholic University of America Press, 1948.

Kent, Homer A., Jr. *Jerusalem to Rome*. Grand Rapids: Baker Book House, 1972.

———. "Philippians." In *The Expositor's Bible Commentary*, volume 11, edited by Frank E. Gaebelein. Grand Rapids: Zondervan Publishing House, 1978.

———. *Treasures of Wisdom: Studies in Colossians and Philemon*. Grand Rapids: Baker Book House, 1978.

Kittel, Gerhard, and Friedrich, Gerhard, eds. *Theological Dictionary of the New Testament*. Translated by Geoffrey W. Bromiley. Grand Rapids: Wm. B. Eerdmans Publishing Co., 1964–72.

Lenski, R. C. H. *Interpretation of First and Second Corinthians.* Columbus: Wartburg Press, 1946.

Luck, G. Coleman. *Second Corinthians.* Everyman's Bible Commentary series. Chicago: Moody Press, 1968.

Metzger, Bruce M. *A Textual Commentary on the Greek New Testament.* London: United Bible Societies, 1971.

Mitchell, Daniel R. "II Corinthians." In *Liberty Commentary on the New Testament.* Lynchburg, VA: Liberty Press, 1978.

Morgan, G. Campbell. *The Corinthian Letters of Paul.* New York: Fleming H. Revell Co., 1946.

Plummer, Alfred. *Corinthians Two.* The International Critical Commentary series. Naperville, IL: Alec R. Allenson, 1915. Reprinted 1975.

Price, Robert M. "Punished in Paradise (An Exegetical Theory on II Corinthians 12:1-10)." *Journal for the Study of the New Testament.* Issue 7 (April 1980).

Ramsay, W. M. *St. Paul the Traveller and the Roman Citizen.* Grand Rapids: Baker Book House, reprinted 1979.

Robinson, Henry S. *The Urban Development of Ancient Corinth.* Athens: American School of Classical Studies, 1965.

Thrall, Margaret E. "The Problem of II Cor. VI.14-VII.1 in Some Recent Discussion." *New Testament Studies* 24:1 (October 1977).

———. "Super Apostles, Servants of Christ, and Servants of Satan." *Journal for the Study of the New Testament.* Issue 6 (January 1980).

Walvoord, John F. "Reconciliation." *Bibliotheca Sacra* 120:477 (January 1963).

Wilson, R. "How Gnostic Were the Corinthians?" *New Testament Studies* 19:1 (October 1972).